ST OSWALD'S WAY AND
ST CUTHBERT'S WAY

LONG-DISTANCE TRAILS IN NORTHUMBERLAND
AND THE BORDERS

About the Author

Rudolf Abraham (www.rudolfabraham.co.uk) is an award-winning writer and photographer whose love of travel and remote places has taken him from the Balkans to eastern Turkey, Central Asia and Patagonia. Guilty for many years of travelling straight through Northumberland en route to the Scottish Highlands, he finally stopped to spend time there in 2008 – and has been returning to his favourite corner of the British Isles ever since.

Other Cicerone guides by the author
The Mountains of Montenegro: A Walker's and Trekker's Guide
Torres del Paine: Trekking in Chile's Premier National Park
Walking in Croatia

ST OSWALD'S WAY AND ST CUTHBERT'S WAY

LONG-DISTANCE TRAILS IN NORTHUMBERLAND AND THE BORDERS

by Rudolf Abraham

CICERONE

2 POLICE SQUARE, MILNTHORPE, CUMBRIA LA7 7PY
www.cicerone.co.uk

Printed by KHL Printing, Singapore.
A catalogue record for this book is available from the British Library.
All photographs © Rudolf Abraham.

For Ivana and Tamara

Advice to Readers

While every effort is made by our authors to ensure the accuracy of guidebooks as they go to print, changes can occur during the lifetime of an edition. If we know of any, there will be an Updates tab on this book's page on the Cicerone website (www.cicerone.co.uk), so please check before planning your trip. We also advise that you check information about such things as transport, accommodation and shops locally. Even rights of way can be altered over time. We are always grateful for information about any discrepancies between a guidebook and the facts on the ground, sent by email to info@cicerone.co.uk or by post to Cicerone, 2 Police Square, Milnthorpe LA7 7PY, United Kingdom.

Front cover: View of Alnmouth from Church Hill across the mouth of the River Aln (SOW, Stage 4)

CONTENTS

Route symbols on OS map extracts	Features on the overview map
route	County/Unitary boundary
alternative/extension	National boundary
adjacent trail	Urban area
start point	National park
finish point	Forest Park/National Forest Area of Outstanding Natural Beauty
alternative start point	
alternative finish point	National Scenic Area
direction of walk	

For OS legend see OS maps.

Abbreviations

The abbreviations used for the main route names in the text are as follows:

- **SOW**   St Oswald's Way
- **SCW**   St Cuthbert's Way
- **NCP**   Northumberland Coast Path
- **NST**   North Sea Trail

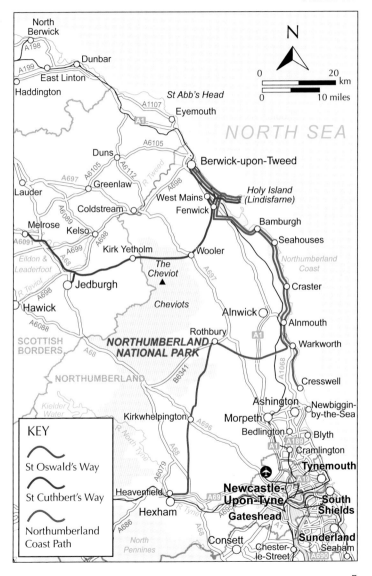

ACKNOWLEDGEMENTS

I would like to thank Jude Leitch, Tourism Development Manager at Northumberland Tourism, for all her help throughout the writing of this guide; Frances Whitehead, Communications Officer at Northumberland National Park; John Gelson at East Coast Trains; Claire Thorburn at Impact PR; Gill Thompson at Northumberland National Park; Iain Robson of Northumberland Coast AONB; Martin Kitching of Northern Experience Wildlife Tours; Michael McCuish of Visit Scotland; Sarah Hindhaugh, Head Gardener at Belsay Gardens; Janet and Bob Young at East Coast B&B; Lorna and Richard Thornton at Cornhills Farmhouse; Mark Kennedy at the Lindisfarne Inn; Marilyn and Jon Bridger of the Farmhouse at Yetholm Mill; Ben McHugh at the Red Lion in Alnmouth; Anne Park at the Tankerville Arms in Wooler; Teresa Wilson at the Queen's Head, Rothbury; Margaret Blackburn at the Border Hotel, Kirk Yetholm; Ann Foggin at Tosson Tower Farm; Julia and Alex Wallace at Glenbank House, Jedburgh; Jim and Catherine Robson at the Station Inn, Hexham; Julie and Sarah Gregory at Springhill Farm; Jon Monk of Shepherd Walks; Ian Clayton, Lifeboat Operations Manager at Seahouses RNLI; Cavan Scott, former editor of *Countryfile*, and Matthew Havercroft, editor of *Discover Britain* (formerly *Heritage*), who sent me off to research and write about Northumberland's winter wildlife and the gardens at Belsay Hall respectively; Ronald Turnbull; Jonathan and all the team at Cicerone; and Terry Marsh, formerly Membership Secretary of the Outdoor Writers and Photographers Guild, who arranged an AGM and Awards Dinner in Northumberland National Park in 2008 and in so doing, inadvertently set this book in motion.

View of Goswick Sands from Cheswick Sands (SOW, Stage 8)

The small walled garden (designed by Gertrude Jekyll in 1911), and Lindisfarne Castle (SOW, Stage 7)

INTRODUCTION

Looking north across the Coquet Valley from Simonside, Northumberland National Park (SOW, Stage 2)

For with the flow and ebb, its style
Varies from continent to isle;
Dry shod o'er sands, twice every day,
The pilgrims to the shrine find way;
Twice every day the waves efface
Of staves and sandalled feet the trace.

Marmion, Sir Walter Scott

I am inclined to think that the Cheviots are the loveliest country in England…There is an extraordinary stillness and peace in their forms; and nowhere in the world is the light and colour of sky and earth more lovely than in this bit of England.

Virginia Woolf's husband, Leonard, writing of their stay in Wooler, Northumberland in 1914

I first visited Northumberland National Park in the late autumn of 2008, spending a memorable weekend near Rothbury, and following a trail up onto the Simonside Hills. As I stood on the craggy sandstone summit, and surrounded by a sea of heather – grazed by feral goats and punctuated by the occasional Iron Age cairn – the low cloud suddenly dissipated to reveal a view stretching out over the Northumberland coast, drenched in mauve and gold and pierced by shafts of sunlight. I have been returning to the area ever since.

Both St Oswald's Way and St Cuthbert's Way are long-distance trails that lead the walker through a beautiful, diverse and at times remote landscape – from farmland to rugged hills, and from sandstone outcrops and heather moorland to enormous sandy beaches and rolling coastal dunes. The routes are enhanced by a wealth of birdlife, and are rich with a staggering amount of historical interest.

St Oswald's Way stretches 97 miles (156km) from Heavenfield, on Hadrian's Wall in Northumberland, to Holy Island (Lindisfarne) on the Northumberland coast, and is described in this guide as continuing up the Northumberland Coast Path to Berwick-upon-Tweed, making a total distance of 110 miles (176.5km). This addition of this last stage provides both superb coastal scenery, and takes advantage of the better transport links in Berwick-upon-Tweed. St Cuthbert's Way stretches 62 miles (100km), from Melrose in the Borders to Holy Island, and again is described in this guide as continuing up the coast to Berwick-upon-Tweed, a total distance of 79 miles (127km).

Both walks pass through Northumberland National Park and the Northumberland Coast Area of Outstanding Natural Beauty (AONB). At times they meet and share routes with other, well-known trails, including the Pennine Way and Hadrian's Wall Path, and St Oswald's Way follows almost the entire length of the Northumberland Coast Path. Indeed, if you follow the route description from Cresswell to Warkworth in this guide (Stage 1 of the Northumberland Coast Path), as well as the section of St Oswald's Way (as described here) between Warkworth and Berwick-upon-Tweed, you will also have completed all of the Northumberland Coast Path. St Cuthbert's Way crosses the ancient, rugged Cheviot Hills, cloaked in pale moor-grass and studded with tors of volcanic rock, as well as the Eildon and Leaderfoot National Scenic Area (NSA); St Oswald's Way crosses one end of the Simonside Hills. Each trail visits some magnificent architecture – rambling castles, Norman churches, medieval abbeys – as well as sites of enormous archaeological and geological interest, quiet villages, Sites of Special Scientific Interest and Special Areas of Conservation – and, come to that, some outstandingly good pubs.

View of the Northumberland coast south of the Skerrs and Cocklawburn Beach (SOW, Stage 8)

Access by public transport is straightforward, trails are mostly well maintained and clearly marked, and the walking itself is easy.

Despite their many charms, St Oswald's Way and St Cuthbert's Way see remarkably few walkers in comparison to most other long-distance trails in the UK. Northumberland National Park not only has the lowest population density of any national park in Britain, but also some of the lowest visitor numbers – a distinction that is both a great pity (because it is an absolutely beautiful area), and at the same time one of its great charms – it is a world away from the crowds of some of Britain's more frequented wild places. Much the same could be said for Northumberland as a whole.

GEOLOGY

During the Carboniferous period, around 360–290 million years ago, the area that would eventually become Northumberland and southeast Scotland was submerged beneath a shallow tropical sea, somewhere near the equator. Ages of deposition of shells and other marine life on the bed of this sea formed layers of limestone, which were then overlaid by vast amounts of mud and sediment from large river deltas. Swamps developed on these deltas and forests grew, and in time the peat and plant debris from these were covered by further layers of sedimentation. Changes in sea level caused this cycle to repeat itself over millions of years, creating the limestone, sandstone, coal and shale that typify the area's landscape today, and the layers of sedimentary rock so evident on the Northumberland coast, folded and faulted over subsequent millennia. Distinctive folds of limestone can be seen at Cocklawburn, between Goswick and Berwick-upon-Tweed, and limestone bands project into the sea nearby as the Skerrs. Inland, the fell sandstone formed during this period can be seen in the Simonside Hills and Harbottle Crags, and in the rocks that form St Cuthbert's Cave; on the coast, sandstone appears at Longhoughton Steel near Boulmer, and south towards Alnmouth.

The single most distinctive geological feature of Northumberland is the Whin Sill. A great elongated sheet of dolerite rock, it was formed when molten rock oozed up through cracks and fissures in the earth's crust then spread out between layers of sedimentary rock, during the end of the Carboniferous period, some 295 million years ago. Its distinctive vertical cracks and columns were formed as the molten rock cooled. The Whin Sill stretches from one side of the county to the other, and upon its hard outcrops are built many of Northumberland's most prominent monuments, including Hadrian's Wall, Lindisfarne Castle and Bamburgh Castle. In the east it splinters off the Northumberland coast in features such as Harkess Rocks near Bamburgh, making its easternmost appearance with the Farne Islands, and its southernmost appearance near Craster, at Cullernose Point. Dolerite is often known as whinstone in Northumberland.

Statue of St Cuthbert by Fenwick Lawson, in the ruins of Lindisfarne Priory, Holy Island (SOW, Stage 7)

Successive periods of glaciation from around 2 million to 12,000 years ago scoured the landscape and shaped it into its present form, leaving the broad, familiar U-shaped valleys, as well as meltwater channels (particularly clear on Humbleton Hill in the Cheviots) and the vast, undulating and mineral-rich deposits that coat much of the landscape today. These glaciers also carried and deposited rocks far from their geological origin – attested by the presence of blocks of volcanic rock from the Cheviots on the Northumberland and Yorkshire coasts. One well-known 'erratic' boulder is the Hunkleton Stone at Newbiggin-by-the-Sea.

Among the oldest geological features in Northumberland are the Cheviot Hills. The Cheviots were formed during the Devonian period, some 380 million years ago, and are the remnants of volcanoes and their huge lava flows, which covered an area of some 230 square miles (600 square kilometres). An enormous mass of granite was later intruded beneath these volcanoes, and it is the upper levels of this granite core, exposed by eons of subsequent erosion, which now form these hills. The volcanic cones themselves have long gone. The heat from these later intrusions 'baked' and further hardened the existing lava with which it came into contact, and it is this metamorphosed rock that forms the familiar rocky tors of the Cheviots. Further north, in the Borders, the Eildons also constitute the remnants of a laccolith or volcanic intrusion.

Sand dunes form a fairly narrow band along parts of the Northumberland coast, the largest and most extensive of these being found at Cheswick Sands and Goswick Sands, and the Snook on Holy Island. While there are some very old dunes based on glacial sands and clays in Lindisfarne National Nature Reserve (Ross Links, for example, on the mainland south of Holy Island, contains some of the oldest dunes in Britain), the majority of sand dunes on the Northumberland coast are relatively young, formed over the last 200–300 years. Due to their age, the older dunes are more acidic, which is reflected in the plant species that grow there. The enormous erosive power of the sea is everywhere apparent as you walk along the north Northumberland coast – perhaps nowhere more so than Alnmouth, where a storm in 1806 blasted through the sand dunes, permanently altering the position of the mouth of the River Aln.

WEATHER

Northumberland's geographical position on the northeast coast of England acts as a moderating influence as far as climate is concerned – meaning that although statistics point to it being on average the coldest county in England, it escapes the extremes of some other areas in the UK.

Vallum (earthworks) at Hadrian's Wall (SOW, Stage 1)

Summer temperatures at Boulmer on the Northumberland coast reach an average daytime high of around 18°C in July and August (the highest recorded in the past two decades was 28.2°C in August 1990), with an average low of 10.8°C for the same months. June and September have average maximum temperatures of 15.6°C and 15.9°C respectively, and average minimum temperatures of 8.6°C and 9.1°C; the same values for May and October are 12.5°C/5.9°C and 12.8°C/6.7°C respectively. January has the lowest average temperatures, with an average maximum of 6.7°C and an average minimum of 1.3°C (although in January 1982 it plummeted to –12.3°C), with February only very marginally higher. May and June see the greatest number of hours of

sunshine, followed by July and August. Average sea surface temperatures on the Northumberland coast are, as might be expected, quite low (around 13°C in summer, compared to 18°C on England's southwest coast).

Inland, temperatures are similar to those on the coast but decrease with altitude – thus upland areas such as the Cheviots and Simonside will be several degrees cooler. Yetholm in the Scottish Borders has an average maximum January temperature of 6°C, and an average January minimum of 1°C. The corresponding values for July and August in Yetholm are 20°C and 10°C. Wind chill must be added to these temperatures, which will make them feel considerably cooler.

Rainfall in Northumberland and the Borders is less than experienced in

Flagstone trail on Simonside, Northumberland National Park, a short distance off St Oswald's Way (SOW, Stage 2)

the northwest of England, with an average annual precipitation of 651mm on the coast, and between 890mm (low-lying areas) and 1145mm (The Cheviot) in Northumberland National Park. In the Borders, Yetholm has an average annual precipitation of 603mm. Compare these figures with the Lake District, which has an average annual precipitation of over 3200mm in some areas. November is usually the wettest month, with an average rainfall of 67.2mm on the Northumberland coast, while July typically sees the least rainfall of the summer months (47.6mm) and August the most (62.1mm). Yetholm usually experiences the heaviest rainfall in October (73mm).

Snowfall occurs mainly in January and February, but snow can fall any time between November and March in the hills, with snow lying on average 10 days a year on the coast, more in the hills.

Winds are for the most part moderate, and gusts rarely reach above 18 knots in the summer – although winds reaching gale force are not unknown, despite being uncommon. The windiest months on the coast are December to March, with average gusts reaching over 30 knots; the calmest months are June, July and August.

Nevertheless, bear in mind that all these figures are averages, and variations can be considerable – so check local weather forecasts (see www. metoffice.gov.uk and www.mwis.org. uk). As an example, in 1993 Wark (a few miles northwest of Heavenfield on St Oswald's Way) experienced a record October low of –10.6°C; and in the winter of 2010 heavy snowfall began in November (around 30cm in one day, including the coast) and continued for several days, with temperatures dipping to around –9°C in Northumberland.

WILDLIFE AND PLANTS

Wildlife

The landscape of Northumberland and the Borders is home to an extraordinarily rich and diverse range of wildlife. Its forests are one of the last strongholds of Britain's native red squirrel population – more than half the entire UK red squirrel population lives in Kielder Forest alone – while otters still live alongside its remote, clear streams and burns, stoats and weasels can be seen scampering among its hedgerows, and roe deer and feral goats wander its rugged hills. Minke whales, dolphins and grey seals can all be seen off the Northumberland coast – even a lone humpback whale has been spotted in these waters, as have basking sharks – while salmon and sea trout swim up its rivers to spawn, and some of its shallow lakes are home to Britain's only native species of freshwater crayfish.

The River Tweed is particularly well known for its salmon, while the Farne Islands are home to one of the most important colonies of grey seals in Europe, some 3000–4000 strong. There is an enormous variety

Donkeys outside the village of Kirk Yetholm in the Borders (SCW, Stage 3)

of birdlife, from raptors to seabirds, waterfowl and waders. The Farne Islands are home to four of the five species of British tern (including Arctic and roseate tern), as well as puffins and guillemots. Eider ducks are found here, too; they are sometimes known locally as 'cuddy ducks', referring to St Cuthbert who is said to have placed the birds under special protection following his sojourn on the Farnes in the seventh century. Other birds you are likely to see on the coast include curlew, Mediterranean gull, kittiwake, razorbill and redshank.

During the winter months, Northumberland becomes a temporary home to numerous species of birds migrating from further north – from Iceland, Greenland, Svalbard and Scandinavia. Some stop here only briefly before continuing their migration; others remain throughout the winter, before returning to their breeding grounds in the frozen north. These winter migrants are to be found in particular in the enormous tidal area south of Holy Island on the Northumberland Coast AONB, Fenham Flats, which forms part of Lindisfarne National Nature Reserve, and nearby Budle Bay. They can be seen here in their thousands – from great skeins of shelduck flying overhead, to huge flocks of grey plover grazing on the tidal flats.

Fenham Flats is home during the winter to no fewer than six internationally important species of wildfowl and wading bird. The pale-bellied brent goose, which arrives from its breeding grounds in the Svalbard archipelago, and for whom this is the only regular wintering site in Britain,

19

WATCHING WILDLIFE

There are numerous places where you have a particularly good chance of spotting wildlife, either on or reasonably close to the routes in this guide:

Aln Estuary This is a good place to spot grey plover during the winter, and terns (including roseate) on the beach to the south during autumn. (On St Oswald's Way and the Northumberland Coast Path.)

College Valley There is a reasonable chance of seeing black grouse and a very good chance of seeing feral goats here. (Leading off St Cuthbert's Way, north of Hethpool.)

Coquet Island Lying about 1 mile (1.5km) off the coast, this is an important breeding ground for seabirds, including Arctic and roseate tern. Boat trips leave from Amble. (On the Northumberland Coast Path and a little over 1 mile (1.5km) off St Oswald's Way.)

Cresswell Pond This small nature reserve and SSSI is just inland from the extensive dune systems of Druridge Bay. (Just off the Northumberland Coast Path, north of Cresswell.)

The Farne Islands The best months to see seabirds (puffins, guillemots, Arctic tern) are May–July, whereas the grey seals have their pups late October–November. Boat trips leave from Seahouses. (On St Oswald's Way and the Northumberland Coast Path.)

Fenham Flats and Budle Bay There is a two-storey hide at Fenham Flats, with views taking in the whole sweep of coastline from the Lindisfarne causeway and Holy Island in the north to Guile Point. (Off-route, around 2 miles (3.5km) south of the Holy Island causeway.)

Greenlee Lough A beautiful area of marshland and reedbeds surround this shallow lake. (Off-route, around 10 miles (16km) west from Wall, and slightly north of Hadrian's Wall Path.)

Harkess Rocks These lie just northeast of Bamburgh. Also known as Stag Rocks, they are good for waders and divers, and wintering seaduck. (On St Oswald's Way and the Northumberland Coast Path.)

Hauxley Nature Reserve At the north end of Druridge Bay, this is a good place for waders and migrants. (Just off the Northumberland Coast Path.)

Newton Pond This is a good place to see migrating waders, just south of Low Newton-by-the-Sea. (On St Oswald's Way and the Northumberland Coast Path.)

is joined by pink-footed and greylag geese, wigeon, grey plover and bar-tailed godwits. The whooper swan (distinguishable from the mute swan by its longer, predominantly yellow bill with a black tip) is another of the winter migrants you might see further inland, sometimes from as early as late October.

Inland, the beautiful heather moorland on Simonside in Northumberland National Park is as good a place as any to see red grouse throughout the winter months, and the much scarcer black grouse can be spotted on the Cheviots, in particular in the College Valley. Other species to look out for in the Cheviots include ring ouzel, whinchat and curlew – the latter forming the logo of Northumberland National Park. Ospreys can also be seen at Kielder

Water – the first chicks born in Northumberland for over 200 years were hatched there in 2009.

Moths including the emperor moth and northern eggar are found on areas of heather moorland, and around half the English and Welsh population of the large heath butterfly is found in Northumberland National Park.

Plants

The extensive dune systems of the north Northumberland coast are colonised by species such as marram grass and ragwort, and in more stable areas can be found flowers, including rest harrow and bloody cranesbill – county flower of Northumberland. Specialised species such as silver-weed and marsh helleborine grow in the dune slacks (hollows behind the dunes which are below the water table

Heather and other plants beside the trail in Shiellow Wood (SOW, Stage 6)

for at least part of the year). Among those species found among the older dunes of Lindisfarne National Nature Reserve is the recently discovered endemic Lindisfarne helleborine.

Areas of whin grassland (so called because of the hard, dense whinstone that lies beneath it) are found along the coast, with species such as lyme grass, common rock rose and maiden pick, while bell heather and sedges grow among areas of coastal heathland. Coastal cliff faces are often rich in mosses and lichens, and also support species such as red fescue and spring squill. Eelgrass grows among the mudflats, and pink thrift appears in spring in areas of saltmarsh.

Invasive species include piri piri burr from New Zealand (found on Holy Island among other places); you can help prevent this spreading further by picking the burrs off your boots and trouser legs rather than inadvertently transporting them to other areas.

Inland from the coast, the upland areas of Northumberland National Park are typified by hardy grasses such as moor-grass and mat-grass, as well as heather – which is particularly widespread on fell sandstone areas such as Simonside, although less widespread on the Cheviots, partly as a result of overgrazing. On Simonside, flagstones have been laid along footpaths to protect adjacent areas of heather and bog from erosion.

Several areas of blanket bog survive in Northumberland National Park, fragile and ancient ecosystems typified by cushions of sphagnum moss, which support species such as sundew and asphodel. Recently, conservation efforts have allowed several areas of bog – formerly drained in the process of land reclamation – to become waterlogged again (by blocking drainage channels), so that plant communities can re-establish themselves.

Woodland mostly takes the form of forestry plantations, many of these planted by the Forestry Commission to provide forestry reserves following the Second World War. Nevertheless, there are still a few, highly prized fragments of the ancient, semi-natural woodland that would have once covered much of this landscape – among them Hareshaw Linn near Bellingham, Holystone in Coquetdale and Harrowbog in the College Valley, all within Northumberland National Park. Species in these areas of natural woodland include oak, ash, juniper, downy birch and wych elm.

The plantations that now dot the landscape range in size from small patches of trees to the enormous Kielder Forest, which covers an area of some 250 square miles (402 square kilometres), making it the largest forest in England. However, in the College Valley, some 55,000 deciduous trees were planted in 1995, constituting the largest new 'native' woodland in England.

There are also a number of historic gardens in the region, foremost among these being the gardens at Belsay Hall.

NORTHUMBERLAND NATIONAL PARK

Northumberland National Park was created in 1956, and covers an area of around 405 square miles (1049 square kilometres) between Hadrian's Wall in the south, Kielder Water in the west, the Cheviots and the Scottish border in the north, and Wooler and Rothbury in the east. Within this area are no fewer than 32 Sites of Special Scientific Interest (SSSIs), including the Cheviot tors and Simonside, 6 Special Areas of Conservation (SACs), 3 National Nature Reserves (NNRs) and a RAMSAR site (wetlands of international importance) at Holburn Lake and Moss, as well as several sites of exceptional historical and archaeological interest.

The landscape of the national park ranges from outcrops of the Whin Sill along the course of Hadrian's Wall to the fell sandstone and heather moorland of Simonside, and from the rugged, rolling Cheviots to shallow freshwater lakes, forest and peat bogs. The highest point in the national park is The Cheviot (815m).

The northernmost national park in England and Wales, Northumberland National Park has the lowest population density of any national park in England and Wales by a significant margin (a total of only around 2000 people, compared to over 42,000 in the Lake District National Park, which covers an area slightly more than double its size). Its annual visitor numbers are equally low – 1.5 million,

Looking across the Aln Estuary to Alnmouth (SOW, Stage 4)

compared to 15.8 million in the Lake District National Park and 9.5 million in the Yorkshire Dales National Park.

St Oswald's Way traverses part of Northumberland National Park southwest of Rothbury, including the Simonside Hills; St Cuthbert's Way crosses it in the north, following a route through the Cheviots between the Anglo-Scottish border and Wooler.

NORTHUMBERLAND COAST AONB

Designated in 1958, the Northumberland Coast Area of Outstanding National Beauty covers an area of around 85 square miles (138 square kilometres), along a narrow, 39-mile (64km) strip of coastline between Berwick-upon-Tweed in the north and the Coquet estuary in the south.

It includes 12 SSSIs (among these Alnmouth saltmarsh and dunes and Bamburgh dunes), 3 Special Protected Areas (SPAs) and 2 SACs, and is a RAMSAR site, while Holy Island (Lindisfarne) and the Farne Islands are both NNRs.

St Oswald's Way follows almost the entire length of the Northumberland Coast AONB, from Warkworth to Berwick-upon-Tweed, while St Cuthbert's Way enters the AONB near Holy Island and then follows the coast up to Berwick-upon-Tweed. The Northumberland Coast Path covers the whole length

of the AONB from Cresswell to Berwick-upon-Tweed.

EILDON AND LEADERFOOT NSA

The Eildon and Leaderfoot National Scenic Area – the Scottish equivalent of an AONB – covers an area of around 14 square miles (36 square kilometres), encompassing the Eildon Hills, Melrose and the valleys of the River Tweed and Leader Water. The Tweed and its catchment area are a SSSI. St Cuthbert's Way crosses the Eildons on its first stage, immediately after leaving Melrose, before following the course of the Tweed for a short distance. The area was designated an NSA in 1980.

HISTORY AND HERITAGE

Stone Age and Iron Age
The earliest evidence of human habitation in the area dates from the Mesolithic Period (Middle Stone Age), mostly in the form of stone tools and delicately worked arrowheads, used by the hunter-gatherers who hunted in its woodlands and grasslands, and fished its coastal waters. On a coastal bluff near Howick one of the earliest and best-preserved Mesolithic roundhouses ever to be found in Britain was discovered, inhabited by early Northumbrians around 7000 years ago.

The Northumberland landscape is exceptionally rich in rock art, including large numbers of the enigmatic

Neolithic rock art: cup-and-ring marks at Lordenshaws (SOW, Stage 2)

although strangely beautiful cup-and-ring markings. There are over 1000 recorded examples of this rock art in Northumberland, much of which was little known or appreciated until comparatively recently. Dating from the Neolithic Period (New Stone Age, around 4500–2000BC, a period marked by the gradual adoption of agriculture and the domestication of livestock), it is scattered widely across the area, with several examples on or close to the route of St Oswald's Way (such as Lordenshaws near Rothbury) and St Cuthbert's Way (for instance Weetwood Moor just outside Wooler, and Doddington Moor to the north of this). The meaning of these markings is unknown – although their placement (near a spring or watercourse, or in an area of upland pasture) appears to have been carefully chosen.

The largest Iron Age fort in Northumberland, Yeavering Bell, is passed on St Cuthbert's Way, between Hethpool and Wooler; and one of the Eildon Hills, just outside Melrose at the beginning of St Cuthbert's Way, was also the site of an enormous Iron Age hill fort. Both were once occupied by the powerful Votadini tribe, an Iron Age people made up of several smaller tribes. Numerous other hill forts, cairns (burial mounds) and cists (stone-lined burial chambers) are dotted across the landscape.

Roman Britain

The preeminence of the Votadini was curtailed by the arrival of the Romans in the first century AD. Over the next 300 years the Romans introduced a period of stability in these borderlands, building a network of roads

ST OSWALD

Oswald was born around AD605, the son of Aethelfrith, King of Bernicia, and Queen Acha of Deira. Following his father's death in 616 at the hands of Edwin of Deira, the young Oswald fled to western Scotland, where he converted to Christianity under the influence of monks from the island of Iona. When Edwin was killed by Caedwalla of Gwynedd and Penda of Mercia, Oswald returned to Bernicia with a small army, confronting them at Heavenfield in 634 or 635. According to the eighth-century historian Bede, Oswald erected a large wooden cross on the eve of battle and asked his soldiers to pray for victory. Their ensuing rout of the combined Welsh and Mercian forces – which greatly outnumbered Oswald's – was subsequently attributed to this act of faith.

Oswald's claim to both crowns enabled him to reunite both Bernicia and Deira into one of the most powerful kingdoms of medieval Britain, Northumbria, its territory stretching as far north as the Firth of Forth. He invited an Irish monk, St Aidan, to found a priory on Holy Island (Lindisfarne) in 635 and help spread Christianity in Northumbria.

In 642, Oswald was killed in battle against his old enemy Penda at Oswestry ('Oswald's Tree') in Shropshire. Penda ordered Oswald's body to be hacked to pieces and his head and arms displayed on stakes, although some of his remains were later recovered by Oswald's brother Oswiu. His head was taken to Lindisfarne, but removed when the monks there fled the Viking raids of the ninth century, and eventually came to rest in St Cuthbert's Tomb at Durham Cathedral. Oswald's reign was particularly significant in terms of the more widespread introduction of Christianity in northern England.

(two of which, Dere Street and the Devil's Causeway, are encountered on the routes in this guide) and, from AD122, Hadrian's Wall. Lying at the southern end of St Oswald's Way, the great string of earthworks, milecastles, forts and turrets that form Hadrian's Wall arguably constitute the most memorable Roman archaeological remains anywhere in the UK.

The Anglo-Saxon period

During the fifth century the Angles (a people from the borderlands between Germany and Denmark) and the Saxons (from northern Germany) invaded Britain, filling the power vacuum created by the departure of the Romans. The Angle King Ida took Bamburgh on the northeast Northumberland coast in AD547, naming his new kingdom in northeast

ST CUTHBERT

St Cuthbert was probably born around AD634, in southern Scotland or Northumbria, and began his ministry at Melrose in about 650. He accompanied Eata, Abbot of Melrose, to establish a new monastery at Ripon in what is now North Yorkshire, then became Prior of Melrose Abbey in 664. Cuthbert travelled widely, preaching the gospels in remote villages and becoming renowned for his piety. Later, in 676, he adopted the life of a hermit, taking up residence on one of the Farne Islands. It was during this period that he is said to have placed eider ducks – which still live on the Farnes – under special protection; for this reason, they are still often called 'cuddy ducks' in Northumberland. In 684 he was elected Bishop of Hexham, but instead accepted the position of Bishop of Lindisfarne – a setting which, by its geographical location just north of the Farne Islands, was evidently much closer to his heart.

Cuthbert died on the Farnes in AD687 and was buried at Lindisfarne. In 875, following Viking raids, his remains were removed by the monks of Lindisfarne, and were later buried at Durham.

Both during his lifetime and after his death, Cuthbert was frequently associated with miracles. According to Bede, his body was found to be miraculously preserved when his coffin was opened 11 years after his death; and the ninth-century king Alfred the Great claimed to have had a vision or dream of St Cuthbert which inspired him in his resistance against the Vikings.

A small book placed in Cuthbert's tomb but removed in the 12th century, known as the St Cuthbert Gospel – one of the earliest surviving intact European books, with one of the earliest surviving intact bindings – was purchased by the British Library in 2012. It is planned that the book will be displayed for equal periods in London and Durham.

England and southeast Scotland Bernicia. Ida's grandson Aethelfrith carved out an enormous territory, but following his death Edwin, prince of the neighbouring kingdom of Deira (between the Humber and the Tees), seized the throne, establishing a royal palace at Ad Gefrin (Old Yeavering, near Kirknewton, and not far from St Cuthbert's Way). Edwin was later defeated by the Mercians, led by a chieftain named Penda, and the Welsh king Caedwalla, in AD633, with Aethelfrith's eldest son taking the throne in Bernicia – although he, too, soon met his end. His brother Oswald defeated Caedwalla and Penda at Heavenfield, near Hadrian's Wall in around 635. Attributing his victory to the Christian faith, Oswald set about introducing Christianity to his kingdom. From his capital at Bamburgh he invited St Aidan, an Irish monk from the monastery on Iona, to Bernicia. Aidan settled with a small group of monks on the island of Lindisfarne (Holy Island), and was later followed by St Cuthbert, prior of the abbey at Melrose. Holy Island was to become one of the most important early centres of Christianity in England, and it was here that the Lindisfarne Gospels – one of the most beautiful medieval manuscripts to have survived to the present day – were created in the early years of the eighth century (search for 'The Lindisfarne Gospels' on www.bl.uk).

It is on these events of the seventh century – the Battle of Heavenfield, Oswald's capital at Bamburgh, Holy Island and St Cuthbert's journey from Melrose – that the routes of both St Oswald's Way and St Cuthbert's Way are based.

From the eighth century Britain witnessed successive waves of devastating Viking raids, the first recorded of these taking place on Lindisfarne in 793. By 866 the Vikings had taken York, installing a puppet king in Bernicia, and in 875 the monks of Lindisfarne Priory were forced to flee Holy Island with the remains of St Cuthbert and other relics. The monks are said to have rested at St Cuthbert's Cave (on St Cuthbert's Way and close to St Oswald's Way), and St Cuthbert's remains were later buried at Chester-le-Street, before finding their final

resting place in Durham Cathedral in 995.

The Medieval period

Uprisings in York, Durham and elsewhere following the Norman conquest led to William the Conqueror laying waste to much of the northeast – so much so that England north of the River Tees was not even included in the Domesday Book of 1086. The Scottish King David I invaded northern England in 1138, and the following year the Anglo-Scottish border was established on the River Tees – although by 1157 Northumberland had been reclaimed by England under Henry II.

From the early 12th century many of the region's great abbeys, sacked or destroyed during the Viking raids of previous centuries, were restored or rebuilt, including Lindisfarne, and new monasteries were built at Melrose, Brinkburn and Hexham. The Church of St Laurence in Warkworth is the most complete Norman building in Northumberland.

John Balliol was installed as the Scottish King in 1292, after several years of interregnum following the death of Alexander III (who left no direct heir), under the 'arbitration' of the English King Edward I. Edward invaded Scotland in 1296, and from this date England and Scotland were plunged into a long, protracted period of conflict, with the border areas suffering frequent damage from passing armies. Berwick-upon-Tweed

The chancel at the 12th-century Church of St Laurence in Warkworth, with its vaulted ceiling (SOW, Stage 3)

passed back and forth several times between English and Scottish rule during this period, and the great abbeys at Melrose and Dryburgh were both sacked in the 14th century. Perhaps not surprisingly, this period also coincided with the building or refortifying of some of the greatest castles in the area, including Warkworth, Dunstanburgh and Alnwick.

In 1377 Henry Percy was made the first Earl of Northumberland. The Percy family, one of the most powerful noble families in northeast England, were descended from William de Percy, who had arrived from Normandy with William I. Perhaps the most famous Percy was the first Earl's son, also called Henry – most of the Percys were called Henry or William

– better known as 'Harry Hotspur'. The Percys supported Henry VI and the House of Lancaster during the War of the Roses in the 15th century, several battles of which were fought in Northumberland, although later the fourth Earl was forced to switch his allegiance to Edward IV and the House of York.

The Tudor period

In 1513 the forces of the Scottish King James IV were defeated at Flodden Field, a few miles north of Yeavering Bell and St Cuthbert's Way, by the English army of Henry VIII. Attacks were made on the Borders in the 1530s, and in the widespread destruction of these campaigns and the 'Rough Wooing' of the 1540s (in which Henry VIII attempted to force

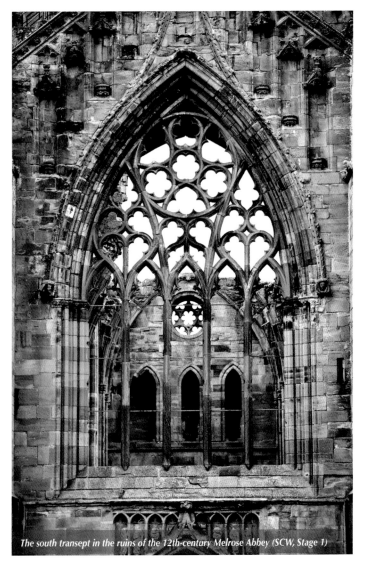

The south transept in the ruins of the 12th-century Melrose Abbey (SCW, Stage 1)

Mary Queen of Scots to marry his son Edward), the abbeys at Melrose and Dryburgh were torched. Henry VIII's dissolution of the monasteries in 1536–1540 sounded the death knell for the other abbeys in this region as elsewhere.

In the 16th century Berwick-upon-Tweed's defences gained an elaborate, Italianate system of bastions and fortifications, the like of which had probably never been seen this far north in Europe at that time, and still constitute the finest Elizabethan fortifications in Britain.

Border Reivers

The instability and frequent devastation experienced by the border regions from the late 13th century onwards – and the hardship this imposed on the area's inhabitants – led to a general state of lawlessness, and the rise of the Reivers. Raiders from both England and Scotland, the Reivers took livestock and other possessions from pretty much anyone not attached to their own family or protected by someone more powerful – a state of affairs that explains the presence of many pele towers and bastles (fortified houses) in the region. The Reivers were transported to Ireland by James VI and I in the early 1600s.

The 18th and 19th centuries

During the 18th and 19th centuries an important lime industry developed in Northumberland, particularly along the coast. The lime was burnt in large brick kilns for agricultural use; initially single or small groups of kilns supplied local farms, but from the late 18th century it was exported by sea (and later by rail), with larger groups of kilns being built, such as those on Holy Island and at Beadnell

Lime kilns by Lindisfarne Castle, Holy Island (SOW, Stage 7)

and Seahouses. Perhaps the best illustration of these kilns in action is a large painting in the entrance hall of Lindisfarne Castle, which depicts the limekilns blazing beside the castle at night. Coal was also mined locally (and used, for example, to fire the limekilns) – the lighthouse at the Snook on Holy Island is said to have been built over a mine shaft. Sandstone was quarried widely, providing stone for local buildings, from farm walls and cottages to bridges, castles and abbeys.

During this period the Northumberland coast experienced a boom in herring fishing, which led to the establishment of processing buildings where the herring was salted and packed for export, as well as smokehouses (one of the few surviving ones is at Craster). The harbour at Seahouses was built specifically to facilitate this herring fishing industry, and purpose-built cottages such as those at Beadnell, Low Newton-by-the-Sea and elsewhere sprang up to house the fishermen. During the early years of the 20th century, as a result of overfishing and with the introduction of steam vessels operating from further afield, herring fishing went into a steep decline.

The First and Second World Wars
The global conflicts of the 20th century have also left their mark on the region. The Otterburn ranges were the site of an elaborate network of trenches, which were dug as a practice area for the trench warfare of the Western Front during the First World War. During the Second World War, the low, flat, open expanses of the north Northumberland coast were one of the suspected points of a projected land invasion by Hitler's Germany – and this part of England

Second World War pillbox near Pauperhaugh on the River Coquet (SOW, Stage 3)

still bears numerous reminders of this period of history.

Pillboxes in various states of preservation are encountered at several points along and just inland from the coast (there are 37 of them within the Northumberland Coast AONB alone), and large concrete anti-tank blocks still lie along the beach between Alnmouth and Warkworth, as well as by the entrance to the Lindisfarne causeway (at Boulmer they were incorporated into the harbour wall). The tidal flats around Holy Island – now part of Lindisfarne National Nature Reserve – were used for live bombing practice, while the remote hilltops of the Cheviots are scattered with the wrecks of Second World War bombers and fighter planes that smashed into their flanks during poor weather or low visibility.

TRANSPORT

The assumption that you need a car to explore the remote areas of Northumberland and the Borders is misplaced, at least for the areas covered by the routes in this guide. While there certainly are places that have no public transport, the trailheads (start/finish points) of St Oswald's Way and St Cuthbert's Way area easily accessible by bus or train, and the towns and villages where you are likely to start/finish the various stages of these walks are well served by local buses. Even a village such as Kirk Yetholm – hardly on the main road to anywhere – has half a dozen buses a day to Kelso, from where there are regular connections to Berwick-upon-Tweed, Edinburgh and other towns in the Borders.

Since St Oswald's Way and St Cuthbert's Way (and for that matter the

To the east of Rothbury, St Oswald's Way follows the course of the former Northumberland Central Railway (SOW, Stage 3)

Northumberland Coast Path) are point-to-point, rather than circular routes, taking a car to the start of the walk would only mean having to return – by public transport – to pick it up after finishing the walk several days later.

The obvious, easiest and certainly the most pleasant way of getting to northeast Northumberland is by train. East Coast Trains (www.eastcoast.co.uk) has fast, regular services between London Kings Cross and Edinburgh, calling at Newcastle and Berwick-upon-Tweed (the finishing point of the routes as described in this guide), with some services stopping at Alnmouth as well. Book in advance to take advantage of discounted online fares.

To get to Heavenfield (for the start of St Oswald's Way), change

at Newcastle, and take a train to Hexham; if approaching from the west, services run from Carlisle to Hexham. From Hexham, buses run to Wall (see below). For further details on rail services see www.nationalrail.co.uk.

Those places not served by rail are easily reached by bus, even off-season. To get to Melrose (for the start of St Cuthbert's Way), there is a service from Berwick-upon-Tweed (67). There are buses from Newcastle to Hexham (685, X85) and Heavenfield (AD122) or Wall (880) for the start of St Oswald's Way. In addition, there are several services running to towns and villages passed on both routes. In particular, the 501 is useful for getting around the towns and villages of the north Northumberland coast, including Alnmouth, Craster and Bamburgh, while the 477 provides an albeit infrequent service for those who wish to get direct from Holy Island to Berwick-upon-Tweed.

For convenience, the main bus services you are likely to use in connection with the routes in this guide are as follows (all services daily unless otherwise specified):

Arriva (www.arrivabus.co.uk)
* 144 (Mon–Sat) Morpeth–Thropton (also stops at Rothbury)

The 12th-century Church of St Laurence in Warkworth, one of the most complete examples of Norman architecture in Northumberland (SOW, Stage 3)

- 501 Berwick-upon-Tweed–Newcastle (also stops at Beal/Holy Island road end, Belford, Bamburgh, Seahouses, Beadnell, Craster, Alnmouth, Alnwick, Felton and Morpeth)
- 505 Berwick-upon-Tweed–Newcastle (also stops at Beal/Holy Island road end and Belford, then A1 direct via Alnwick, also stopping at Felton and Morpeth)
- 518 Newcastle–Alnwick (also stops at Morpeth, Warkworth and Alnmouth)
- 685, X85 and 85 Newcastle–Carlisle (also stops at Hexham) and Newcastle–Hexham
- 714 (May–October, Sun and bank holidays only) Kirkwhelpington–Newcastle

Glen Valley Tours (www.glenvalley.co.uk, tel: 01668 281578) and **Perryman's Buses** (www.perrymansbuses.co.uk, tel: 01289 308719)
- 267 Berwick-upon-Tweed–Wooler (via Etal)
- 464 Berwick-upon-Tweed–Wooler (via Lowick)

Munros of Jedburgh (www.munrosofjedburgh.co.uk, tel: 01835 862253)
- 51 Jedburgh–Edinburgh (also stops at Ancrum and St Boswells)
- 68 Jedburgh–Galashiels (also stops at Ancrum and St Boswells)
- 81, 81A and 81C (Mon–Sat) Kelso–Yetholm (also stops at Morebattle)

- 131 (Mon–Sat) Jedburgh–Newcastle (also stops at Kirkwhelpington)

Perryman's Buses
- 67 Berwick-upon-Tweed–Melrose (also stops at St Boswells)
- 477 (Wed and Sat) Berwick-upon-Tweed–Holy Island (also stops at Beal/Holy Island Road end)

Alba Travel and **Classic Coaches** (www.hadrians-wall.org)
- AD122 'Hadrian's Wall Bus' (April–October) Newcastle–Carlisle (also stops at Hexham and Wall)

Tyne Valley Coaches/Snaith's Travel
- 880 (Mon–Sat) Hexham–Wall

Tynedale Links
- 74 Hexham–Newcastle (also stops at Great Whittington)

These details were correct at the time of writing; however, always check locally for possible changes either to routes or service providers.

For timetables see individual bus company websites or go to www.northumberland.gov.uk and click on *Parking, Roads & Transport* followed by *Experience Northumberland by bus*. For further information on bus and rail services see Traveline (www.traveline.info, tel: 0871 200 22 33).

ACCOMMODATION

Accommodation on and around the routes in this guide is provided by a good range of B&Bs, inns and small hotels, some of them outstanding. Some B&Bs can also provide evening meals and packed lunches by prior arrangement, otherwise there is usually a decent (or, more often, excellent) pub or inn nearby. There are a few Youth Hostels, but not enough to base either of the routes on (even the Youth Hostel at Kirk Yetholm on St Cuthbert's Way, at the end of the Pennine Way, closed in 2011).

Camping is somewhat limited: with the exception of the northern part of the coast, there are not really many campsites on the main routes and camping is prohibited in Northumberland National Park. Prices on Holy Island are generally higher than elsewhere on the coast, and some places require a minimum three-night stay. Despite the fact that Northumberland is often described as England's 'best-kept secret', it pays to book well in advance, especially on the coast in the summer – on some stages there are only a few places providing accommodation.

Suggestions of places to stay are given in the introduction to each stage, which can in most cases be considered a personal recommendation; Appendix D lists further accommodation options.

ABOUT THE ROUTES

No technical difficulties are encountered on either St Oswald's Way or St Cuthbert's Way, and both walks can safely be described as easy. There are no high-level or exposed sections. Some of the stages are quite long,

Walkers in Harwood Forest (SOW, Stage 2)

however, and some of the stiles can be quite steep. The crossing of Gains Law and Humbleton Hill in the northern Cheviots on St Cuthbert's Way could cause navigation problems in low cloud or poor weather, and both these areas, as well as Simonside on St Oswald's Way, can be exposed to strong winds.

St Oswald's Way is the longer of the two routes, stretching 110 miles (176.5km), including continuing the route from Holy Island up the coast to Berwick-upon-Tweed; by comparison St Cuthbert's Way covers 79 miles (127km), again including the route from Holy Island to Berwick-upon-Tweed. St Cuthbert's Way is marginally the higher of the two routes, crossing the Cheviots and reaching 368m on Wideopen Hill – although St Oswald's Way is not far behind, with Coquet Cairn standing at a little over 300m, followed by the heather moorland of Simonside. On both routes there is the possibility of making short detours to higher ground – Simonside on St Oswald's Way (429m) and Mid Eildon on St Cuthbert's Way (422m). Whereas St Oswald's Way is entirely within Northumberland, around half of St Cuthbert's Way is in the Borders. Both routes cross areas of Northumberland National Park (Simonside in the case of St Oswald's Way, the Cheviots in the case of St Cuthbert's Way). St Oswald's Way includes more of the coast, following almost the entire length of the Northumberland Coast Path. In terms of architectural heritage

they are pretty even, with the border abbeys being visited on St Cuthbert's Way, and a succession of castles and abbeys on St Oswald's Way.

You may encounter a few unfamiliar words and place names while walking St Oswald's Way and St Cuthbert's Way, drawn from the rich local dialects in Northumberland and the Borders, some of them Anglo-Saxon in origin (see Appendix B).

WHEN TO GO

The routes in this guide can be walked at any time of year. However, as noted above, the weather is generally at its finest from May to July, and as a result this period together with August sees the largest number of visitors. December and January are usually the wettest months – although sustained periods of fine weather are not impossible in January, both on the Northumberland coast and inland in Northumberland National Park. Winter walking over snow-covered hills can be extremely beautiful for those suitably prepared, although recent winters have seen fairly extreme snowfall, which effectively shut down the local infrastructure, including public transport, and resulted in enormous snow drifts and obliterated trails.

Although Northumberland National Park and other places on St Cuthbert's Way and St Oswald's Way receive fewer visitors during peak season than the Lake District, the same cannot be said about some parts of Hadrian's Wall and Holy Island, which in summer can get rather busy.

Some businesses close out of season – Harestanes Visitor Centre, for example, is open April–October, whereas Melrose Abbey, Lindisfarne Priory and Warkworth Castle are open all year, but with reduced days/hours in the winter. Some B&Bs close for a brief period in November, December or January, but this varies from place to place.

Wildlife and birdlife can be seen throughout the year, although certain species are only present in specific months or seasons. Late spring and summer (May–July) are the best seasons for seabirds on the coast and the Farne Islands; winter migrants arrive in October or November. If you are planning to take a boat over to the Farne Islands, the grey seals have their pups late October–November.

Heather moorland is perhaps at its most beautiful in August, and in late autumn deciduous forest will be a kaleidoscope of reds and golds (indeed some would argue that this is the best season to visit one of the most spectacular gardens in the area, at Belsay Hall).

It is worth bearing in mind the dates of the lambing season (April–May) and the grouse season (August–December). Be careful not to disturb livestock in the former; during the latter, some hotels can be booked out by shooting parties.

WHAT TO TAKE

The clothing and equipment you take depends largely on what season you

St Oswald's Way trail markings near Lordenshaws (SOW, Stage 2)

choose to visit, and will be similar to that required for walking in other upland areas of Britain. A waterproof shell (Gore-tex or similar) is mandatory at any time of year, as are layers of warm clothing (lightweight base and mid layers, and a warm/windproof fleece jacket or similar), lightweight trousers, hat and gloves, and good quality, comfortable walking boots and socks. Outside the summer months you should bring warmer trousers, and gaiters and trekking poles if walking in winter snow. Maps, compass, sunblock, an emergency 'space' blanket and a whistle for attracting attention, and a small first aid kit (including fabric plasters and stretch bandage for sprains and blisters) are other essentials. Make sure you carry sufficient water and food – while some stages pass villages with shops or pubs, others do not, in which case you will need to carry enough for that day.

WAYMARKING AND ACCESS

The routes described in this guide are for the most part clearly marked with a series of distinctive waymarkings, displayed on stiles or gateposts, marker poles and signposts and the like. In the few cases where these are not displayed, the trail is clearly marked with public footpath signs. As a general rule, the waymarkings for St Cuthbert's Way are the clearest and most frequent; those of St Oswald's Way slightly less frequent; while those

Waymarkings for St Cuthbert's Way and the Northumberland Coast Path

of the Northumberland Coast Path/ North Sea Trail can be rather faded at times (although some of these are currently being replaced, see below).

St Oswald's Way is waymarked by round badges with the symbol of a raven (according to legend, a raven was the companion and messenger of St Oswald) and the shield or banner of Northumberland (based on a reconstructed banner of St Oswald); often the raven is replaced by an arrow. **St Cuthbert's Way** is waymarked by a St Cuthbert's Cross. The **Northumberland Coast Path** 'shares' the trail markings of the **North Sea Trail**, a stylised blue letter 'N'. The section of St Oswald's Way that overlaps with the

Northumberland Coast Path was in the process of having a new, combined trail marking added in late 2012.

Other prominent waymarkings you will encounter at certain points on these trails include those of the Pennine Way (an acorn) and the Border Abbeys Way (an amalgamated 'A' and 'W').

Memorial cross in front of the ruins of Lindisfarne Priory, Holy Island (SOW, Stage 7)

MAPS

The routes in this guide are covered by both the OS Explorer (1:25,000) and OS Landranger (1:50,000) series, as follows:
- **St Oswald's Way** OS Explorer OL43, OL42, 325, 332, 340, with Berwick-upon-Tweed just off the latter on 346; OS Landranger 87, 81, 75.
- **St Cuthbert's Way** OS Explorer 338, OL16, 340, with

TREADING LIGHTLY

- Keep to marked footpaths and other rights of way wherever possible, and avoid increasing erosion or damage to adjacent areas. Sand dunes, heather moorland and peat bogs all constitute fragile ecosystems, easily damaged by even the most well-meaning feet.
- Carry all of your litter with you, and dispose of it responsibly in a town or village.
- Do not pick flowers or disturb wildlife.
- Leave gates as you found them.
- Do not disturb livestock, particularly during the lambing season (April–May).
- Keep dogs on a lead when crossing farmland and during breeding season for ground nesting birds (April–July).
- Do not light open fires.

Berwick-upon-Tweed just off the latter on 346; OS Landranger 73, 74, 75.

- **Northumberland Coast Path** OS Explorer 325, 332, 340, with Berwick-upon-Tweed just off the latter on 346; OS Landranger 75, 81.

There is also a series of six sheets covering St Oswald's Way (available from Alnwick County Council or Shepherd Walks); and Harvey's has a map of St Cuthbert's Way (1:40,000), as well as a sheet covering the Cheviots (1:25,000).

All maps in this guide are based on the OS Landranger series (1:50,000). If you want more detail, the OS Explorer sheets are the ones to get.

HILL AND COASTAL SAFETY

The routes described in this guide are for the most part fairly low level; however, the Cheviots and other upland areas require the same precautions as any other upland area in the UK. Low cloud can make route finding (which under good weather conditions would be perfectly easy) more challenging, and occasional screaming winds can make it difficult to stand up, let alone walk in a straight line. The winters of 2009 and 2010 saw extremely heavy snowfall, which began as early as late November (2010) and fell continually for several days, leaving deep drifts in the hills and even on the rocks and beaches of the Northumberland coast laying a carpet of snow some 30cm deep.

Refuge box on the Pilgrim's Route across the sands to Holy Island (SOW, Stage 7)

Always carry waterproof clothing and sufficient warm clothing, a torch, first aid kit, whistle (for attracting attention in an emergency), map and compass (and know how to use them) or a GPS, an emergency or 'space' blanket, and adequate water and food. Follow local weather forecasts. Be alert for traffic on sections of road walking – not that there is likely to be much, but country lanes are narrow and sometimes have little in the way of a grass verge to step onto; and when crossing the East Coast main railway line near Belford (St Oswald's Way) and Fenwick (St Oswald's Way and St Cuthbert's Way), call the signalbox from the phone provided and wait for clearance.

It is essential that you check the safe crossing times for the walk across the sands to Holy Island (or for that matter if crossing by road along the causeway). You need to allow at least 1hr to cross the sands from the first refuge box at South Low (the distance from the mainland to South Low then over the sands to Chare Ends is a little over 2½ miles (4.5km) – some advise allowing up to 2hrs if the sand is soft), and you can only cross the sands safely during the middle of the safe crossing period. Ideally you should aim to *complete* your crossing by the midpoint of the crossing period. Tides may also be influenced by strong winds and other adverse weather conditions. You are strongly advised not to attempt crossing in the dark; besides the danger posed by the tide, accidentally straying from the correct route carries the additional hazard of quicksands and unexploded ordnance.

Safe crossing times for Holy Island are available online from Northumberland County Council (go to www.northumberland.gov.uk and click on *Leisure, Tourism & Culture* followed by *Holy Island Tide Times*) and are prominently and very clearly displayed at the entrance to the Holy Island causeway – so there really is no excuse for 'accidentally' crossing outside these times. Nevertheless the RNLI, usually in conjunction with an RAF helicopter from Boulmer, has been required to make around 60 rescues over the past ten years, of motorists (and only a very small number of walkers) stranded by the tides while crossing to or from Holy Island.

EMERGENCIES

The routes in this guide south of the Scottish border fall within the geographical area covered by NESRA (North East Search and Rescue Association, www.nesra.org.uk), one of the nine regional organisations belonging to Mountain Rescue England and Wales (www.mountain. rescue.org.uk). NESRA acts as an umbrella body for the seven local Mountain Rescue Teams across North Eastern England. The two local teams covering the area relevant to this guidebook are Northumberland National Park Mountain Rescue Team

Walking on the beach near Alnmouth (SOW, Stage 4)

(www.nnpmrt.org.uk, tel: 01912 763312), and North of Tyne Search and Rescue Team (www.northof tynesearchandrescue.org.uk).

In an emergency **dial 999 or 112** and ask for Police, then Mountain Rescue. Calls are then routed to the police control room in the area of the incident (and if required, to another emergency service such as ambulance service or air ambulance). It is important to provide as much information as possible about the accident, the location and nature of the terrain. Be prepared to give the following information:

- Casualties (number, names, ages if known, type of injuries, plus your name)
- Hazards to the rescuers (such as strong winds, rock fall, dangerous animals)
- Access (name of area and description of terrain, and weather conditions if relevant)

- Location of the incident (ideally a grid reference or GPS reference, otherwise a description including any obvious features; map sheet number if known; and specify whether reference is from a map or a GPS)
- Equipment at the scene (torches, mobile phones, warm clothing, emergency shelters)
- Type of incident (what happened, time and apparent cause of incident).

North of the border, the area relevant to this guide (namely the first half of St Cuthbert's Way) is covered by the Border Search and Rescue Unit (www.bordersar.org.uk), one of the teams that make up the Mountain Rescue Committee of Scotland (www. mrcofs.org). The procedure for calling for help in an emergency is the same as that described above – dial 999 or 112 and ask for Police, then Mountain Rescue.

If stranded by the tide or in other emergencies on the Northumberland coast, dial 999 or 112 and ask for the Coastguard (www.rnli.org.uk).

USING THIS GUIDE

As St Oswald's Way and St Cuthbert's Way overlap when they reach the coast, and both routes are described here in the same direction (west to east), the sections where the two follow the same route are not repeated. Therefore, those walking St Cuthbert's Way will need to switch to the route description for St Oswald's Way for the final stages.

The guide uses OS mapping, more specifically the Landranger (1:50,000) series. These should be perfectly sufficient for walking these routes, although if you want to explore the area further, the OS Explorer (1:25,000) series is recommended.

Distances in this guide are given in miles as well as kilometres; elevation is given in metres. The route timings given are an estimate based on a walker of average fitness level; timings do not include stops for rest, lunch or visiting sites passed along the routes.

Within the route descriptions R and L are used for right and left, and N, S, SE (and so on) for compass bearings. References to L and R river banks indicate 'true' left and right, in other words they assume you are looking downstream.

For the sake of brevity, abbreviations have also been used for the main route names in the text, as follows:

SOW	St Oswald's Way
SCW	St Cuthbert's Way
NCP	Northumberland Coast Path
NST	North Sea Trail

For other long-distance footpaths that are only mentioned or encountered briefly (for example the Border Abbeys Way and the Pennine Way) their full title has been used.

'The Journey', Fenwick Lawson's wooden sculpture of monks from Lindisfarne carrying the body of St Cuthbert as they flee Viking raids (SOW, Stage 7)

ST OSWALD'S WAY

Moon above Lordenshaw Hill, site of an Iron Age hill fort (Stage 2)

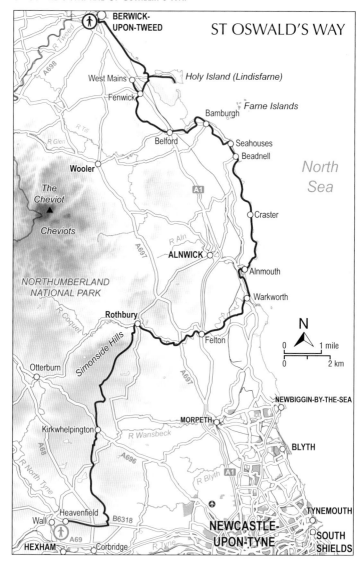

INTRODUCTION

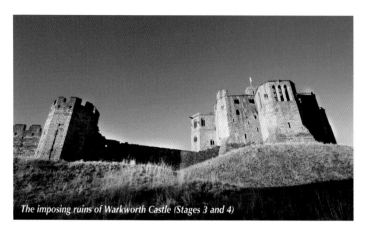

The imposing ruins of Warkworth Castle (Stages 3 and 4)

St Oswald's Way opened in August 2006, its route based on that of a walk devised by the Embleton Church Council. The route stretches 97 miles (156km), linking sites associated with the life of St Oswald, the seventh-century Anglo-Saxon king who was largely responsible for the introduction of Christianity in northern England. Stretching from Heavenfield, near Hadrian's Wall, to Holy Island (Lindisfarne), off the north Northumberland coast, it traverses landscapes ranging from rolling farmland to heather moorland, weathered sandstone crags and some of the most beautiful coastal scenery anywhere in the UK. Quiet fishing villages and market towns are interspersed with spectacular castles,

Neolithic rock art and incredibly rich birdlife.

The standard route description for St Oswald's Way is divided into six stages (days) of between 13½ miles (21.5km) and 19 miles (31km) each. However, you might want to add to this getting to or from Heavenfield (an additional 1½ miles (2.5km) from Wall, or 4½ miles (7.5km) from Hexham); and you will almost certainly want to continue along the Northumberland Coast Path from Holy Island to Berwick-upon-Tweed (an additional 10½ miles (17km) from the Holy Island causeway, or around 13 miles (20.5km) from Holy Island itself), rather than walking back to West Mains along the road and waiting for a bus.

Walking on the beach between Warkworth and Alnmouth, with Coquet Island in the distance (Stage 4)

This makes a grand total of 110 miles (176.5km) or 111½ miles (179km) (from Heavenfield or Wall respectively to Berwick-upon-Tweed), which in this guide is spread over eight days, as follows:

- **Stage 1** Heavenfield to Kirkwhelpington – 17½ miles (28.5km), or 19 miles (31km) if starting from Wall
- **Stage 2** Kirkwhelpington to Rothbury – 15 miles (24km)
- **Stage 3** Rothbury to Warkworth – 18 miles (29km)
- **Stage 4** Warkworth to Craster – 13½ miles (21.5km)
- **Stage 5** Craster to Bamburgh – 14 miles (22km)
- **Stage 6** Bamburgh to West Mains/Fenwick – 14½ miles (23.5km)/13 miles (21km)

- **Stage 7** West Mains/Fenwick to Holy Island – 6 miles (9.5km)
- **Stage 8** Holy Island to Berwick-upon-Tweed – 13 miles (20.5km)

There is scope for shortening or lengthening these stages, to walk the route in fewer days (say, seven days minimum, by walking Stages 6 and 7 in one day) or more (the world's your oyster). You might also consider spending an aditional half or full day (that is, two nights) on Holy Island or based at West Mains, to explore Holy Island properly. Bear in mind that there is no accommodation at intermediate points on or near the route on Stages 1 and 2 (or more specifically between Hadrian's Wall and Knowesgate, and Knowesgate and Rothbury). From here on, however (Rothbury to Berwick-upon-Tweed), there are plenty of opportunities for walking shorter stages (for example stopping at Weldon Bridge or Felton on Stage 3, Alnmouth or Boulmer on Stage 4).

The route is usually described east to west (from Holy Island to the approximate site of the Battle of Heavenfield), in other words in the opposite direction to that given here. In this guide, however, it is described from west to east, simply because this gives a walk to the coast and Holy Island through scenery that becomes increasingly beautiful.

For reference, the 'standard' route (Holy Island to Heavenfield) is usually divided as follows:

- **Stage 1** Holy Island to Bamburgh – 19 miles (31km)
- **Stage 2** Bamburgh to Craster – 14 miles (22km)
- **Stage 3** Craster to Warkworth – 13½ miles (21.5km)

- **Stage 4** Warkworth to Rothbury – 18 miles (29km)
- **Stage 5** Rothbury to Kirkwhelpington – 15 miles (24km)
- **Stage 6** Kirkwhelpington to Heavenfield – 17½ miles (28.5km)

Walkers can apply for a certificate after completing St Oswald's Way, but will need to have purchased a certificate pack (which can be ordered from Shepherd Walks, www.shepherdwalks.co.uk). The pack includes a sheet for making rubbings from the raised motif at the corner of six information panels found along the route, as proof of completion.

For more details about transport options and getting around see Transport in the main introduction.

Sheds made from boat hulls, with Lindisfarne Castle in the distance (Stage 7)

STAGE 1

Heavenfield to Kirkwhelpington

Start	Wooden cross, Heavenfield, or 880 bus stop, Wall
Finish	Post office, Kirkwhelpington
Distance	17½ miles (28.5km) from Heavenfield; 19 miles (31km) from Wall
Time	8hrs 15mins or 8hrs 45mins
Maps	OS Explorer OL42, OL43 and 316; OS Landranger 87 and 81
Access	East Coast Trains to Newcastle, followed by a train to Hexham; or if approaching from the west, by rail from Carlisle to Hexham. From Hexham take the AD122 bus to Heavenfield. Alternatively (or outside April to October, when the AD122 does not run), take the 880 to Wall, and walk N on the A6079 to pick up Hadrian's Wall Path just outside the village. Turn R onto Hadrian's Wall Path, crossing the B6320 at Planetrees Farm. Otherwise it is only a short taxi ride from Hexham to Heavenfield (www.advancedtaxis.com, tel: 01434 606565).
Accommodation	Cornhills Farm B&B, near Knowesgate. There is no alternative accommodation at any intermediate point between Hadrian's Wall and Knowesgate.
Note	There are no SOW trail markings until leaving Hadrian's Wall Path.

This is an easy day, following Hadrian's Wall Path initially then crossing farmland with a gentle climb over Todridge Fell, and visiting several villages. The route entails paths and tracks with a fairly long (but not uninteresting) stretch of road walking. Although it is possible to walk from Hexham to Heavenfield at the beginning of this stage, this makes it a very long day – 22 miles (36km) – with only one potential place to shorten the stage, and that is in the first part of the day anyway.

Before heading to Heavenfield, it is well worth visiting Hexham Abbey. The priory church (now the parish church of St Andrew) was built in the 12th century, on the site of an earlier seventh-century church (which later became a cathedral, until the bishop moved to Lindisfarne) damaged by Viking raids. The crypt survives largely intact from the original seventh-century building, and the stone chair upon which the bishop once sat can still be seen inside the church.

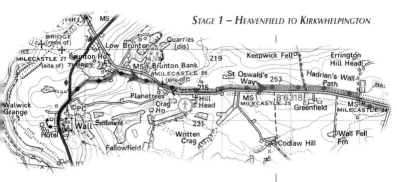

Heavenfield, at the south end of SOW, marks the approximate site of the Battle of Heavenfield, in which Oswald son of Aethelfrith defeated King Caedwalla of Wales and Penda of Mercia in around 635, and regained the crown of Bernicia and Deira (Northumbria). Oswald erected a large wooden cross at Heavenfield, and is said to have asked his soldiers to pray before battle. The present wooden cross dates from the 1920s, and replaced an earlier stone one. There is an annual pilgrimage from Hexham Abbey to the small 18th-century Church of St Oswald in Heavenfield, on or around 5 August.

Hadrian's Wall was mostly built in AD120–130 under the Roman Emperor Hadrian. It stretches some 80 Roman miles – that is, around 73 miles (117km) – between Wallsend on the River Tyne in the east and Bowness-on-Solway in the west. More than simply a 'wall', it was a highly complex barrier consisting of a stone wall fronted on the north by a V-shaped ditch, a series of milecastles, forts and turrets (connected by a metalled road, the Roman Military Way, much of it now the B6318), and a broad series of earthworks and ditch to the south (the Vallum), together with a number of outlying forts. (The Vallum is particularly well preserved on the section of SOW just east of the A68.) Its function is thought to have been administrative as much as defensive, its numerous gates acting as

Map continues on page 52

*Vallum (earthworks)
at Hadrian's Wall*

customs posts for the collection of taxes. For much of its course the wall follows the Whin Sill, making use of its many rocky outcrops. Hadrian's Wall remains one of the best-preserved and complex Roman frontiers in the world, and was inscribed on the UNESCO list of World Heritage Sites in 1987 (www.hadrians-wall.org).

Follow signs for Hadrian's Wall Path E from **Heavenfield**, passing St Oswald's Hill Farm and walking parallel to and just N of the B6318. After around 1½ miles (2.5km), cross with care to the S side of the road, walking through the edge of Stanley Plantation to reach the junction with the **A68**.

Dere Street was a Roman road running between the Firth of Forth, near Edinburgh, and York (where it connected with the Roman road running south to London and Dover), and was probably constructed around AD80. At this point (and elsewhere) its course is hidden beneath the A68, although some other sections are not and are clearly defined on the landscape. One such section of Dere Street is followed on St Cuthbert's Way, near Jedburgh.

Cross the A68 (Roman Dere Street, if you prefer) by the **Errington Arms** (the last accommodation on or near SOW until Cornhills Farm at the end of the stage) and continue along Hadrian's Wall Path on the S side of the B6318. Just after passing a small area of woodland you walk past a particularly well-preserved section of the Vallum. Cross to the N side of the B6318, then just after **Carr Hill Farm** turn L (N) onto a footpath marked SOW.

Map continues on page 57

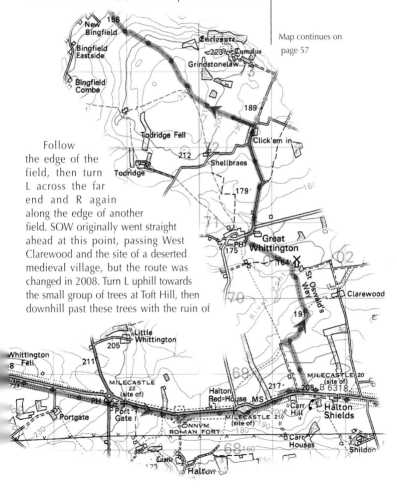

Follow the edge of the field, then turn L across the far end and R again along the edge of another field. SOW originally went straight ahead at this point, passing West Clarewood and the site of a deserted medieval village, but the route was changed in 2008. Turn L uphill towards the small group of trees at Toft Hill, then downhill past these trees with the ruin of

The remains of Whittington Mill, an 18th-century windmill near the village of Great Whittington

Whittington Mill ahead. Turn L then cross the bridge over the **River Pont** to reach Whittington Mill, the impressive remains of an 18th-century stone windmill. Follow the path NW from the windmill to arrive at the village of **Great Whittington**.

> **Great Whittington** is an attractive little village just west of Matfen, with mostly 19th-century stone housing and a small Methodist chapel, now a private house. The pub here (The Queen's Head) would be a useful option for accommodation, but was closed at the time of writing. The 74 bus stops in Great Whittington.

Turn R onto the road, following it round to the L, then straight ahead. Around 1 mile (1.5km) from Great Whittington, you pass **Click-Em-In Farm** – immediately after this turn L onto a track signposted to Bingfield Combe. Keep straight ahead, crossing the so-called Devil's Causeway – another Roman road, this time running from Dere Street near Corbridge to the mouth of the River Tweed near Berwick-upon-Tweed (this is also passed on St Cuthbert's Way near East Horton). Just before the crest of the hill turn R onto a path (no SOW markings), cutting across the corner of a field near the channel of a small stream. Follow the edge of the field to the R then turn L through a gate, and R alongside the edge of the field. After another gate veer diagonally across a field with the highest point of Todridge Fell and Duns Moor (222m) on your L. ▶

The stile on the far side of the field is not obvious at first, being hidden in a slight depression just to the R of a stone wall. Descend alongside this wall, passing some sort of small quarry pit on your R. Veer L then R around the edge of a small plantation, then descend alongside a wall to reach a road.

Follow the road to the R then L, to reach a crossroads by a **war memorial**. Keep straight ahead, to reach the village of **Hallington**.

There are good views from here over the Tyne Valley to the S; the strip of water ahead of you to the NW is Hallington Reservoir.

Whittledean Watercourse (from Hallington Reservoir) running beside Hallington Hall

Hallington is a small settlement, consisting of little more than a farm and the rather grand Hallington Hall. Hallington Hall was built in 1768 for Ralph Soulsby, although it was modified later in the 18th century and mid-19th century. To the northwest are a series of four reservoirs, built between 1863 and 1880 for the Newcastle and Gateshead Water Company; Hallington East and Hallington West are the two nearest, with Little Swinburne and Colt Crag Reservoirs beyond. Together they form an important wintering area for wildfowl. The Whittledean Watercourse, running alongside Hallington Hall, carries water away towards Newcastle.

Follow the road out of Hallington, alongside a narrow strip of woodland and a moss-covered stone wall. At the far end of the trees, Hallington East and West Reservoirs are visible on your L, then after passing another area of woodland **Dovecot Hill** (the 'dovecot' of which once formed part of the landscaped gardens of Bavington Hall) comes into view on your L. Shortly after, you arrive at the main road (**B6342**). Turn R onto this (caution required!) to arrive at the village of **Little Bavington**.

Bavington Hall, just to the east of Little Bavington, was built in the late 17th century for the Shafto family, although altered and extended in the 18th century for its subsequent owner, Admiral Delaval. It was once surrounded by extensive landscaped gardens – of which little remains except the 'dovecot' already passed on Dovecot Hill, actually an eye-catcher in the form of a miniature castle.

At the far side of the village turn L onto a footpath – the end of this long section of road walking, you may be pleased to learn. Descend alongside a row of trees, cross the small bridge over the stream then head diagonally across the field to join a farm track, passing a small plantation on your R. Turn L onto a path just before a gate, ascending with a wall on your R and Bavington Crags (an outcrop of the Whin Sill) on your L. Turn L at **Clay Walls Farm**, briefly following the edge of a small plantation then turning R through this and L over fields to join the asphalt farm track a little way beyond the farm buildings. Turn L onto the farm track, then where it descends to the R keep straight ahead to arrive at the village of **Great Bavington**.

Great Bavington – as its name suggests – was once somewhat larger than the small village you see today. It probably lost its prominence due to poor harvests and outbreaks of plague in the 14th century – although traces of former houses, which existed

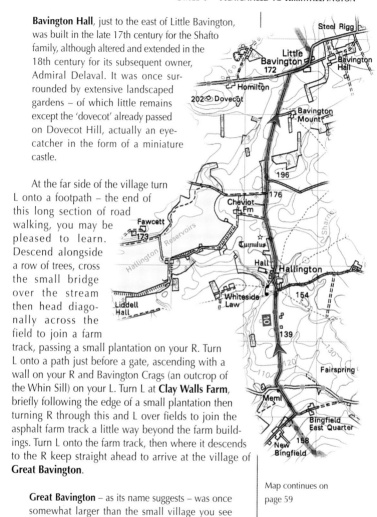

Map continues on page 59

Victorian postbox in the wall of what was formerly the village school, part of the oldest building in Great Bavington

until the 18th century, are visible in the fields to the northeast. After passing the church on your left – dating from 1725 and originally Presbyterian (making it the third oldest Presbyterian congregation in England), but now United Reformed Church – turn left into a narrow lane. The house on the right with a Victorian postbox used to be the village school; after 1946 it was a Youth Hostel – closed, we are told, on account of the 'unseemly behaviour' of its guests. The house beyond it, also on the right, was formerly a pub called The Harvest Home. Together these two houses form the oldest building in the village, dated 1625. Opposite them is a house called the Manse, where Kathleen Raine, the English poet and scholar on William Blake, spent part of her childhood during the First World War, as recalled in her autobiography *Farewell Happy Fields* (1973).

Go straight ahead from the village, over a cattle grid, then immediately after this veer R off the sealed road bearing NNE on a rough farm track. The area of Bavington Crags on the L is a designated SSSI due to its rare plantlife,

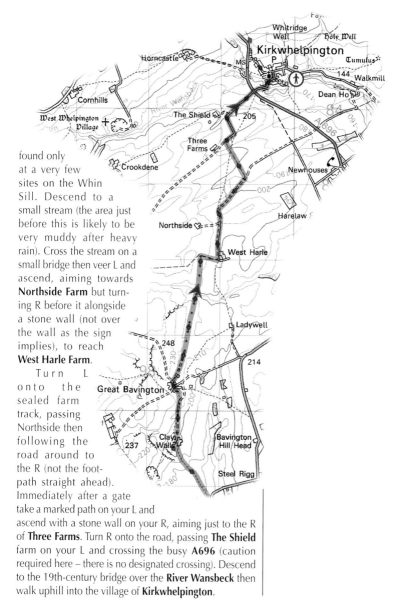

found only at a very few sites on the Whin Sill. Descend to a small stream (the area just before this is likely to be very muddy after heavy rain). Cross the stream on a small bridge then veer L and ascend, aiming towards **Northside Farm** but turning R before it alongside a stone wall (not over the wall as the sign implies), to reach **West Harle Farm**.

Turn L onto the sealed farm track, passing Northside then following the road around to the R (not the footpath straight ahead). Immediately after a gate take a marked path on your L and ascend with a stone wall on your R, aiming just to the R of **Three Farms**. Turn R onto the road, passing **The Shield** farm on your L and crossing the busy **A696** (caution required here – there is no designated crossing). Descend to the 19th-century bridge over the **River Wansbeck** then walk uphill into the village of **Kirkwhelpington**.

KIRKWHELPINGTON

The Church of St Bartholomew in Kirkwhelpington dates from the 13th century, and many details from this date remain despite some restoration in the late 19th century. The interior includes a 17th-century font sitting on top of a reversed 14th or 15th-century capital, and stained glass by Heaton, Butler and Bayne, one of the leading stained glass firms of the 19th century. Among the gravestones in the churchyard is that of Sir Charles Parsons (1854–1931), inventor of the steam turbine, who is buried here with his wife.

About 3 miles east of Kirkwhelpington is Wallington Hall, home of the Trevelyan family, often frequented by the Victorian poet Algernon Charles Swinburne (www.nationaltrust.org.uk/wallington).

Although there is currently no accommodation in Kirkwhelpington itself, Cornhills Farm B&B (www.northumberlandfarmhouse.co.uk, tel: 01830 540232), just off-route near Knowesgate, picks up walkers (either from Kirkwhelpington or Knowesgate) and drops them back there in the morning – and also provides excellent, home-cooked evening meals. If you have time, continue as far as Knowesgate, an additional 1¼ miles (2km), and ask to be picked up there, which will give you a slightly shorter day tomorrow or allow more time around Simonside. The Knowesgate Inn, at Knowesgate itself, suffers from a very poor reputation. The 714 and 131 buses stop in Kirkwhelpington.

Cornhills Farmhouse B&B

STAGE 2
Kirkwhelpington to Rothbury

Start	Post office, Kirkwhelpington
Finish	Market cross, Rothbury
Distance	15 miles (24km)
Time	6hrs
Maps	OS Explorer OL42; OS Landranger 81
Access	The 714 bus from Newcastle and Gateshead stops at Kirkwhelpington (May–October, Sun and bank holidays only); the 131 Jedburgh–Newcastle stops at Kirkwhelpington (Mon–Sat)
Accommodation	The Queen's Head, Rothbury and several alternatives in Rothbury; Tosson Tower Farm just off-route if exploring Simonside further.

This lovely day of walking, partly through Northumberland National Park, takes in the vast expanse of Harwood Forest and the outstandingly beautiful heather moorland and fell sandstone of Simonside. Using good paths and forest tracks, it passes some fascinating Neolithic rock art before finishing in the attractive old market town of Rothbury.

Walk N from the post office in **Kirkwhelpington**, turning L past the bus stop then following the road round to the R. Just before reaching the main road, take a marked footpath on the R. This soon descends to the verge by the A696, then almost immediately veers R again, away from the road and uphill, passing earthworks that include medieval ridge and furrow marks. Pass **West Whitehall Farm**, then turn L onto the road and descend towards the junction of the A698 and the road to Cornhills Farm at Knowesgate, but before you reach the junction turn R onto a track.

> The name **Knowesgate** is derived from the word knowe (pronounced 'now'), meaning hill. The course of the Wansbeck Valley Railway, built in the 1860s but now dismantled, runs through Knowesgate, where there was a station.

Veer R, then leave the farm track by a small plantation. Head just E of N across a field on a not particularly clear trail to the R of a small low hill, aiming for the group of small

Map continues on page 65

plantations around Catcherside (not the plantation next to the A698). Cross a boggy area (possibly easier further L) then cross a stile on the R side of the field, then another near the corner of a wall. Head diagonally down through a field towards the L corner of the

Looking towards the Simonside Hills from Coquet Cairn on the edge of Harwood Forest

nearest plantation, crossing a bridge over a small burn. Just to the NW of here is **Camp Hill**, site of an Iron Age hill fort. Turn R through a gate and alongside the plantation, then switch to the L side of the second plantation and follow the wall at the far end of this up to **Catcherside Farm**. ◀

Veer R then L at the farm buildings, then turn R down a farm track alongside another two plantations. Turn R at the N end of the second, narrow plantation and follow its edge, with views of Harwood Forest on your L. Turn R just before **Fairnley Farm**, then L beside a small plantation, and descend L towards an obvious bridge over the **Ottercops Burn**. Go through a gate then L uphill just to the R of the fence (do not go diagonally over the field to the far corner of Harwood Forest). Turn L onto the road, then turn R onto the road leading into **Harwood Forest**.

> **Harwood Forest** was planted in the 1950s by the Forestry Commission, on what had previously been farmland, to provide reserve timber following the Second World War. It covers an area of 3500ha and is dominated by densely planted Sitka spruce (*Picea sitchensis*) with smaller stands of Lodgepole pine (*Pinus contorta*). Several areas have been felled and replanted since the 1990s, creating open vistas to the surrounding landscape, and the areas around watercourses monitored for plants and wildlife. The Whiskershiel Burn on the SE edge of Harwood Forest is a SSSI.

Ignore the track on your L, keeping straight ahead, then walk through the small settlement of **Harwood**. Go over a crossroads then pass another track on your L and one on your R. Turn R at the next track, with SOW trail markings and signposted to Redpath (there is no 'short-cut' as marked on the OS sheets). Pass another trail on your R then emerge into an open area of felled trees interspersed with new growth, with the farmhouse at Redpath visible ahead of you, and Simonside in the distance. About 45mins after entering Harwood Forest, you arrive at **Redpath** farmhouse.

The farm cottage here was originally a bastle – a defensive house with thick walls and a living area above a barn for livestock.

Turn R onto a marked path just after the farmhouse, and follow this into the trees. Follow marker poles and trail markings (the trail is not always clear at first), then along a clear path, keeping above the edge of the forest and passing a ruined stone sheepfold on your L. Emerge into an open area, crossing a small stream, with the **Fallowlees Burn** on your R. Ascend into the trees again, then turn R onto the forest track. Pass alongside another felled area (not yet marked as such on the OS sheets) to reach **Fallowlees Farm**.

Turn L by the farmhouse then R onto a marked path, alongside a stone wall, then L through the trees. Emerge into another felled area, marshy at first then along a winding path with stones piled onto tree trunks marking the way. Go straight ahead over the forestry track, descend a path, then turn L onto the track again. Cross the bridge over the **Newbiggin Burn**, with Lough Hill on your L, then follow the track uphill. After a short distance turn R onto a path (marked as a bridleway), following this to reach the edge of Harwood Forest at **Coquet Cairn**.

At just over 300m, **Coquet Cairn** marks the highest point on SOW (unless of course you decide to make a

detour onto Simonside), and the view north, of the long ridge of the Simonside Hills rising

Map continues on page 67

65

above a sea of heather moorland, is among the finest on the entire walk. To the east, Druridge Bay is visible on the Northumberland coast.

Follow the path and boardwalks across the moorland, veering R to a stile (not straight ahead through the gate in the direction of Simonside's high point). Descend to the pretty **Forest Burn**, which runs through a small area of deciduous woodland, then ascend and keep R. Cross a second arm of the woodland surrounding the Forest Burn, then pass a small plantation on your L to arrive at **Spylaw Farm**.

Turn R onto a track alongside a small area of tree plantings, then take the L of two stiles. Keep straight ahead on a broad path, with no SOW markings, aiming just to the R of the Simonside ridge and passing the deep peat of Caudhole Moss, veering L where the trail splits and crossing over the E shoulder of **Simonside**.

Near the summit of Simonside, Northumberland National Park

Simonside

Simonside is one of the most beautiful areas of Northumberland National Park, and those who have time are strongly encouraged to follow the trail on the left up

to its summit (429m), passing the Beacon and the wind- and ice-sculpted outcrops of **Dove Crag** on the way, then retrace your steps (allow an additional 45mins each way). Simonside's extensive heather moorland, blanket bog and deep peat areas (the peat reaches some 10m deep at Caudhole Moss) have earned it the status of a SAC and a SSSI. Wildlife includes rare species such as large heath butterfly and mountain bumblebee, and feral goats can sometimes be seen near the summit area.

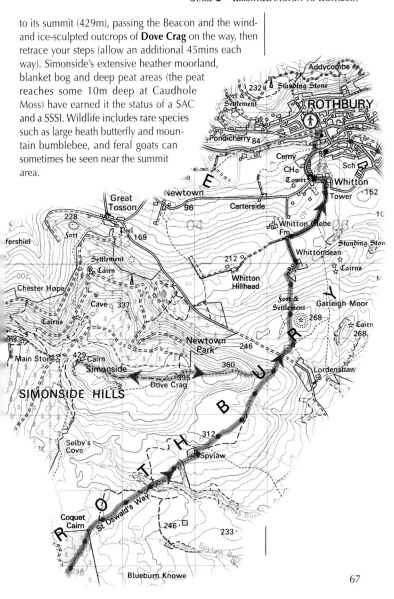

There are several burial cairns on and around Simonside, and stones with Neolithic cup-and-ring marks hidden in the area of forest to the north. In local folk-lore Simonside has associations with fairyfolk and mischievous dwarfs (the Duergar) who try to lead benighted travellers astray, preferably over a lethal crag (all the more reason to carry a headtorch). Tosson Tower Farm B&B, 1½ miles (2.5km) to the north, is well placed for exploring the area further (www.tossontowerfarm.com, tel: 01669 620228).

Descend to the car park at **Lordenshaws**.

Lordenshaws is the site of several examples of Neolithic rock art, stones bearing cup-and-ring marks (see History and heritage). The main stone is just to the left of the main trail after leaving the car park, with a further stone just beyond it; to the right is an Iron Age hill fort, and another stone beyond this. There are also the remains of a wall from a medieval deer park.

Follow the clear trail N from Lordenshaws, passing the main cup-and-ring marked stone on your L and the **hill fort** on your R, then descend on a clear path, passing

Sharp's Folly, an 18th-century tower (built by the Vicar of Rothbury and used as an observatory)

a pond to reach the cottages at **Whittondean**, and turning L through a gate next to one of the houses. Go straight ahead on an unsealed road, then R onto another road, passing Sharp's Folly (an early 18th-century tower built by the Vicar of Rothbury, and used as an observatory), then L onto an asphalt road at **Whitton**. The 14th-century tower house at Whitton was built as home to the vicars of Rothbury. Turn R at the junction and walk downhill past the hospital, then turn L at the car park, crossing the footbridge over the River Coquet to reach the centre of **Rothbury**.

ROTHBURY

Rothbury is a small, peaceful market town sitting astride the River Coquet. It was probably founded in Anglo-Saxon times (it has been suggested that the name derives from that of a local Anglo-Saxon chieftain). The market cross, which dates from 1902 and is in the Arts and Crafts style, was erected as a memorial to Lord and Lady Armstrong, who lived at Cragside. The nearby All Saints Church dates from the 13th century but was almost entirely rebuilt in the 19th century, although traces of the earlier church can be seen in the chancel. Nothing remains of an earlier Anglo-Saxon church that once stood here, but the present church does contain a fragment of an Anglo-Saxon cross, which forms the base of a 17th-century font. The old bridge was built in the 15th century, with a fourth arch added in the 18th century, and the top unfortunately smothered in concrete during the 20th century. At the time of writing work is being carried out on the bridge to remove the concrete elements and possibly reinstate the stone parapets.

Just to the east of Rothbury is **Cragside**, the impressive home of the first Lord Armstrong, wealthy Victorian inventor and industrialist. The house itself is the late 19th-century creation of the architect Norman Shaw, and is surrounded by extensive gardens and woodland (Armstrong planted many of the trees himself), as well as five manmade lakes and one of the largest rock gardens in Europe. It was also the first house in the world to be lit by hydroelectricity.

Accommodation in Rothbury includes the Queen's Head (www.queens headrothbury.com, tel: 01669 620470), which also has excellent food, and Springfield B&B (www.springfieldguesthouse.co.uk, tel: 01669 621277). There is a supermarket on the High Street, and the number 144 bus stops opposite the Queen's Head.

STAGE 3
Rothbury to Warkworth

Start	Car park on the R (S) bank of the Coquet, Rothbury
Finish	Market square, Warkworth
Distance	18 miles (29km)
Time	8hrs
Maps	OS Explorer 325 and 332; OS Landranger 81
Access	The 144 (Mon–Sat) Morpeth–Thropton bus stops at Rothbury
Accommodation	Warkworth House Hotel and several alternatives in Warkworth. At intermediate points, accommodation is available at Weldon Bridge and Felton.

This is an easy but long day of walking along the valley of the River Coquet, with a surprising amount of up and down, along paths, a disused railway line and farm tracks, passing areas of semi-native woodland, several attractive bridges and including glimpses of Brinkburn Priory.

Map continues on page 73

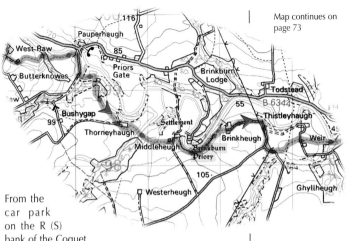

From the car park on the R (S) bank of the Coquet in **Rothbury**, walk E on the main road, passing the bridge (if you have stayed at the Queen's Head or elsewhere on the High Street, you can simply follow the High Street down to the bridge), before turning L onto Wagtail Road. Turn R just before **Wagtail Farm**, through the remains of a bridge, passing a small shed made from old railway sleepers and crossing a bridge over the Whitton Burn.

> You are now following the course of the dismantled **Northumberland Central Railway**, a single-gauge line built in the 19th century between Rothbury and Scots Gap. It stopped running in 1963.

After walking through a rocky gully with the remains of an old footbridge overhead, turn L and follow the path across the field, passing a deserted cottage on your L. At **West Raw Farm**, turn R onto a track then L onto a path, bearing L just after an abandoned cottage then R across a field with a plantation on your L. At the end of the field, follow a path through the trees above a stream on your R, then into a field and R alongside the **River Coquet**, to arrive at the 19th-century bridge at **Pauperhaugh**. ▶ Turn

Note the two outer, land arches, included with flood conditions in mind.

18th-century stone bridge over the River Coquet at Pauperhaugh

R onto the road, passing a World War II pillbox in the field on your R – the first of many you will see on the route to Berwick-upon-Tweed.

Turn L off the road, cross a bridge, then L and follow the edge of the wood around to the R. Turn R at an abandoned cottage and follow the steep path to the top of the hill, then turn L, through a gate (but not L over a stile) and walk above the Coquet with a fence on your L. Look back to your R for views of the Simonside Hills. At **Thorneyhaugh Farm** keep straight ahead, descending steeply and crossing the footbridge over the **Maglin Burn**, then steeply uphill again and straight ahead to **Middleheugh Farm**. Follow a path to the R of the farmhouse, then R uphill alongside a plantation, with glimpses of **Brinkburn Priory** below.

Brinkburn Priory, on a secluded bend in the River Coquet, was founded in the 12th century for Augustinian canons, and restored in the 19th century. Since it lies on the north bank of the river it cannot be accessed from SOW (access is from the

B6344 between Pauperhaugh and Weldon). It can be visited April–November (search for it on www. english-heritage.org.uk).

Follow the edge of the plantation, then go straight ahead through the farm buildings at **Brinkheugh Farm**, and along a farm track. Follow the track to the R then turn L at the road junction, and L onto a path just before reaching a bridge. Go straight ahead across a lane, aiming for the R-hand corner of the field (not L downhill), then cross a footbridge over the **Todd Burn**. Walk past the **weir** and follow the R bank of the Coquet to the road, then turn L and follow this over the bridge into the village of **Weldon**.

Weldon Bridge was built around 1804, replacing two earlier bridges washed away by flooding in the mid-18th century. Note the circular opening between two of the arches, to allow flood waters through. The Angler's Arms, an 18th-century coaching inn, offers food and accommodation (www.anglersarms.com, tel: 01665 570271).

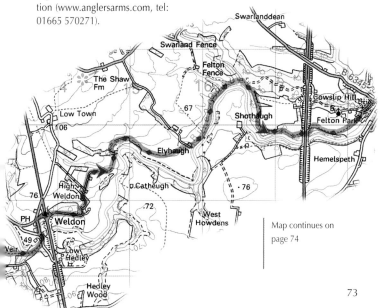

Map continues on page 74

Follow the road uphill beside the Angler's Arms, cross the main road with care (there is no crossing) and follow it to the R, under the A697. Take a track on your L and turn L just before reaching a house, following a path around the back of the house then up through more houses at **High Weldon**. Go straight ahead on a track, then L uphill on a path just before reaching a house. Follow the path through woodland then along the edge of a field above the Coquet, to reach **Elyhaugh Farm**. Pass the farmhouse on your R, then

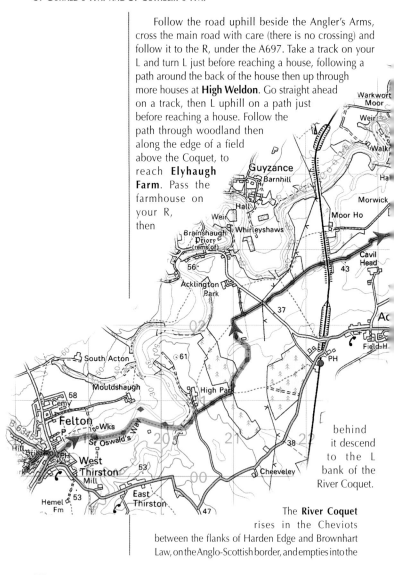

behind it descend to the L bank of the River Coquet.

The **River Coquet** rises in the Cheviots between the flanks of Harden Edge and Brownhart Law, on the Anglo-Scottish border, and empties into the

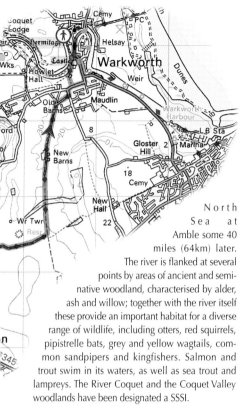

North Sea at Amble some 40 miles (64km) later. The river is flanked at several points by areas of ancient and semi-native woodland, characterised by alder, ash and willow; together with the river itself these provide an important habitat for a diverse range of wildlife, including otters, red squirrels, pipistrelle bats, grey and yellow wagtails, common sandpipers and kingfishers. Salmon and trout swim in its waters, as well as sea trout and lampreys. The River Coquet and the Coquet Valley woodlands have been designated a SSSI.

St Mary's Church at Felton Park, on the outskirts of Felton

Follow the path through fields, ascending and descending then crossing the bridge over the **Swarland Burn**. Go uphill and bear R on a track through woodland, keeping R and passing under the A1. Cross a field, with the prominent spire of St Mary's Church on your L at **Felton Park**, to arrive on the edge of **Felton**.

FELTON

The village of Felton sits on the north bank of the Coquet, at the point where the old Great North Road (the old coaching route between London and Edinburgh) crossed the river. Facing it on the opposite bank is the village of West Thirston. The old bridge between the two probably dates from the 15th century, and is now restricted to pedestrian use, with traffic crossing on the adjacent (and unhappily, quite unattractive) 'new' bridge, built in the 1920s. Felton Mill, on the southwest side of the village, was the last working mill in Northumberland, and one of the county's largest. One of the houses nearby (6 Riverside) probably dates from the 16th century.

The Church of St Michael and the Archangels is a striking building, much of it dating from the 12th–14th centuries, although the chancel roof was added in the 19th century along with some other alterations. Nearby Felton Park was burnt to the ground by the English King John in the 13th century, since it was here that the Northern barons had met to discuss allegiance to the Scottish King Alexander II rather than paying taxes to King John; later it was a base for the Jacobite Rebellion in 1715.

Accommodation in Felton includes River Cottage B&B (www.river-cottage-bandb.co.uk, tel: 01670 787081). The 501 and 505 buses stop in Felton.

Pass the Church of St Michael of the Archangels on your L and follow the road downhill, then turn R, passing the war memorial to reach the bridge over the River Coquet.

Cross the bridge and turn L alongside the Coquet, following a track and then a path alongside a beautiful section of river bank. Cross the bridge over the sidestream and follow the track uphill towards **High Park Farm** (no waymarkings initially), bearing L and then R, then L again just after a plantation. Follow the edge of the plantation, then bear L, taking a track on your L then bearing R. Keep straight ahead over a road and go under the East Coast

railway line to reach the road into Warkworth, just S of **Morwick Dairy Farm** (where the famed local Morwick Dairy Ice Cream is made, www.royaldouble.com). Turn L onto the road then R onto another track, then L through a plantation to reach **New Barns Farm**, and straight ahead into Warkworth.

Warkworth Castle's magnificent cross-shaped keep crowns a hilltop above the River Coquet

Turn R onto the main road then L to reach the old town centre, passing Warkworth's magnificent castle on the way. The path goes to the L of the castle, but the views are actually at their best from the entrance and from the road to the right of it. Either way, it is under 10mins' walk to **Warkworth** market square.

WARKWORTH

Warkworth has a well-preserved old centre enclosed within a tight bend in the River Coquet, with Castle Street running downhill from the castle to the market square. Warkworth Castle was built in the 12th century, and some parts of the original building, such as the gatehouse, still remain. The impressive keep, which was built after the castle was given to the Percy family and is the castle's most intact building, dates from the 14th century (search 'Warkworth Castle and Hermitage' on www.english-heritage.org.uk). Down by the river and accessible only by boat is Warkworth Hermitage, an elaborate chapel and sacristy cut into the sandstone rock around 1330–1340, with adjacent living quarters dating from the 15th century.

The Church of St Laurence, just north of the market cross, is the most complete Norman building in Northumberland, and contains one of the few vaulted 12th-century chancels of any church in England, richly decorated and reminiscent of Durham Cathedral. The effigy of the knight in the south aisle is from the 14th century, and there are fragments of medieval stained glass at the eastern end of the south aisle. The market cross dates from around 1830, although its octagonal base is earlier. The old bridge (now just for pedestrian use) dates from the 14th century, and has a fortified tower at one end.

Accommodation includes the Warkworth House Hotel (www.warkworthhousehotel.co.uk, tel: 01665 711276), near the old bridge. The number 518 bus stops at the market square in Warkworth.

The base of the old market cross in Warkworth, with emblems of the Percy family

STAGE 4
Warkworth to Craster

Start	Market square, Warkworth
Finish	Harbour, Craster
Distance	13½ miles (21.5km)
Time	5hrs 20mins
Maps	OS Explorer 332; OS Landranger 81
Access	The 518 Newcastle–Alnwick bus stops at Warkworth
Accommodation	Harbour Lights B&B in Craster; alternatives in nearby Dunstan village. At intermediate points, accommodation available at Alnmouth and (more limited) Boulmer.

An easy day of walking, on clear paths and sandy beaches, either just inland of the dunes or, for some sections (tide permitting), along the beach itself. It takes you past the lovely village of Alnmouth as well as Boulmer. NCP and NST signs complement, and sometimes replace, those of SOW from here on.

From the market square in **Warkworth**, walk N passing the Church of St Laurence (which is definitely worth a visit) on your R, then turn R alongside the River Coquet. Turn L and cross the old bridge, then immediately R and follow the road uphill. Keep straight ahead (do not take the minor road on your R at the top of the hill) then straight ahead on a footpath at the entrance to the caravan park and follow this down past the golf course to the dunes, and the broad swath of pale sand beach that stretches up to **Marden Rocks**, beyond Alnmouth Bay.

To the SE is **Coquet Island**, a SSSI managed as an RSPB reserve, where birdlife includes puffins and roseate terns (boat trips are possible from Amble during the summer, although landing on the island itself is prohibited). The island (which is limestone, and does not form part of the Whin Sill) was probably a monastic site from the seventh century, and

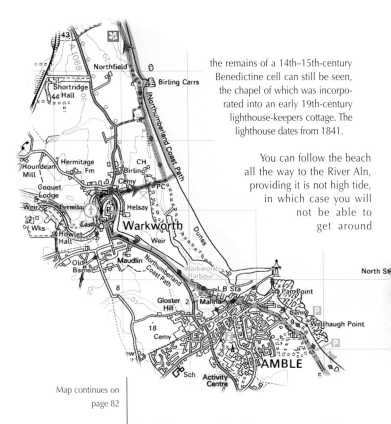

the remains of a 14th–15th-century Benedictine cell can still be seen, the chapel of which was incorporated into an early 19th-century lighthouse-keepers cottage. The lighthouse dates from 1841.

You can follow the beach all the way to the River Aln, providing it is not high tide, in which case you will not be able to get around

Map continues on page 82

the **Birling Carrs**, although you can turn inland just to the S of them if this is the case. It is a lovely stretch of beach, and makes a fine introduction to the next few stages of walking along the coast. If it is high tide or if you prefer not to walk along the beach, you can turn L just before reaching the beach and follow the path just behind the dunes, alongside the golf course then L by the footbridge (there is access to the beach at this point) and R onto a track. Follow the track through the caravan site (after which there is access to the beach again, then a path through the sand dunes (part of Alnmouth dunes and saltmarsh SSSI) before turning inland on a track, as described below.

As you walk along the beach you pass a long row of **anti-tank blocks**, part of the defensive system laid down along the northeast coast in the Second World War, when this was a suspected point for a land invasion by Hitler's Germany. There are more blocks at the entrance to the Holy Island causeway (Stages 7 and 8), and old World War II pillboxes, in various states of preservation, will be encountered at various points along SOW over the next few days.

Concrete anti-tank blocks from the Second World War, on the beach between Alnmouth and Warkworth

Coquet Island
NORTHUMBERLAND
outh Steel

If following the beach (arguably the more attractive route), turn L at the mouth of the **River Aln**, but do *not* attempt to cross it at this point – although you are only a stone's throw from Alnmouth, you need to allow around 1hr to walk around the estuary (it is, however, an interesting walk with excellent views). Walk around the headland (or if the tide is too high you can walk over Church Hill instead) and S alongside the mature saltmarsh of the Aln Estuary – this is the largest area of this habitat on the NE coast, which along with the adjacent sand dunes and their important plant communities has been designated a SSSI. Pass a small, roofless mortuary chapel dating from

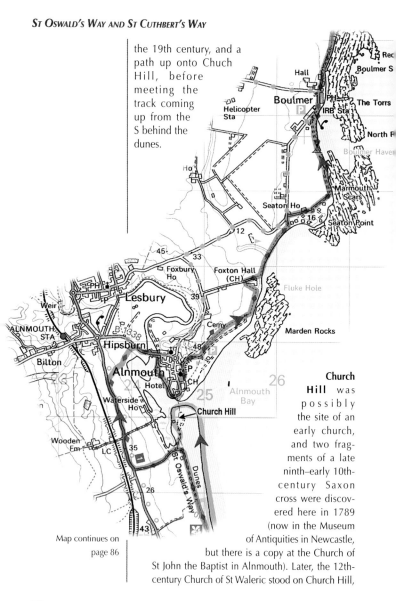

the 19th century, and a path up onto Chuch Hill, before meeting the track coming up from the S behind the dunes.

Church Hill was possibly the site of an early church, and two fragments of a late ninth–early 10th-century Saxon cross were discovered here in 1789 (now in the Museum of Antiquities in Newcastle, but there is a copy at the Church of St John the Baptist in Alnmouth). Later, the 12th-century Church of St Waleric stood on Church Hill,

Map continues on page 86

82

although what little of that remained by the 19th century was obliterated by the great storm of 1806. There are excellent views across the Aln to Alnmouth.

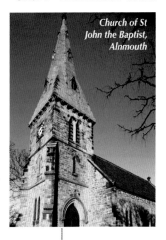

Church of St John the Baptist, Alnmouth

Whether you have followed the beach or the track behind the dunes, turn onto a track leading inland (W) from the salt-marsh, passing a path on your R which leads along the edge of the marshes to a bird hide, although the path is prone to flooding. Turn R just before the road (**A1068**) and follow the cycle track, with good views of Alnmouth and its estuary on your R. Go straight across a road leading down to the estuary (there is no access to Alnmouth from there) then follow the cycle route R down towards the River Aln. Cross the 19th-century bridge, then immediately turn R through a white gate onto a footpath, marked 'Lovers Walk' and with the Coast Path sign. ▶

This brings you around the edge of a tidal estuary, with views of pretty painted houses across the field on your L, to arrive in **Alnmouth**. Keep alongside the estuary for SOW, or turn L up Garden Terrace and onto Northumberland Street for shops, pubs and accommodation.

For those joining the route at Alnmouth rail station: follow the road downhill from the station, to reach the roundabout in about 15mins, where you join SOW and the NCP.

The village of Alnmouth viewed across the mouth of the River Aln

ALNMOUTH

The far (southern) end of Alnmouth overlooks the coast and the tidal estuary of the River Aln, and on the far side of the latter, Church Hill. The landscape here might look fairly timeless, but in fact a little over 200 years ago it looked very different: Church Hill was once attached to the village of Alnmouth, but in 1806 a particularly violent storm broke through the sand dunes, altering the course of the River Aln which since that date has flowed into the sea between Church Hill and Alnmouth itself. The harbour gradually silted up, spelling the end of Alnmouth's days as a port.

There is a replica of the cross from Church Hill just inside the door of the pretty late 19th-century parish church of St John the Baptist, a short distance along Northumberland Street, the dim, wood-beamed interior redolent with the smell of timber.

Alnmouth has several pubs, including the Red Lion (www.redlion alnmouth.com, tel: 01665 830584), which has a small, friendly bar, excellent food and real ales. It also has some lovely, spacious guestrooms. Other accommodation in Alnmouth includes Beaches B&B (www.beachesbyo. co.uk, tel: 01665 830006). There is also a small deli, café, grocers, gift shops and a post office. The 501 and 518 buses stop in Northumberland Street, opposite the Red Lion.

Head down to the golf course, turn L, then R onto the marked footpath over the edge of the golf course (or R down the road just past this). Turn L at the car park, walking alongside the golf course, then veer L over the headland, along the edge of the golf course and then along a partly overgrown path at the end. Turn L (watch out for golf balls!) just before Foxton, then around the back of **Foxton Hall**, and down a concrete drive to rejoin the coast, turning L onto the beach. ◄

Note the warning sign here regarding the tide, which can come very high up the beach.

Towards the far end of the beach, turn L up the concrete steps, then R through caravans and holiday cottages or bungalows. Turn L then R on a farm track, passing the farm buildings and through a gate, then slightly L on the track (not the path ahead), along a path just above the beach. Look out for the two navigation posts, which incoming boats need to line up in order to safely navigate Mar Mouth, the narrow entrance to Boulmer Haven between the lethal rocks of North and South Reins. Just

over 3 miles (5km) from Alnmouth, you
arrive in the village of **Boulmer**.

Very much the traditional
Northumberland fishing village,
Boulmer (pronounced 'Boomer')
appears to have changed little over the
past hundred years or so, despite the
arrival of the RAF base a short distance
inland during the Second World War.
Crab, lobster and sea salmon are still
brought ashore from small open fishing
boats (cobles) in the rock-enclosed shelter of Boulmer Haven. Food and accommodation (three nights minimum) are
provided by the Fishing Boat Inn (www.
thefishingboatinn.co.uk, tel: 01665
577750). The annual village fete is held
on the Saturday of August Bank Holiday
weekend.

*'Barmy owl' sculpture
on wall near the
village of Boulmer*

During the 18th and 19th centuries Boulmer
was the centre of a notorious smuggling trade –
in particular gin – with much of this illicit activity
being planned at the Fishing Boat Inn. One of the
most notorious characters in this illicit trade was
Will Faa, King of the Yetholm Gypsies, who lived
in Kirk Yetholm just over the Scottish border on St
Cuthbert's Way.

Continue along the road through the village, passing the bus stop, and the **Fishing Boat Inn** on your R.
Go straight ahead along a farm track at the far end of the
village, as Dunstanburgh Castle comes into view ahead.
Note the three metal bird sculptures on the wall on your
L, made by local farmer Geoff Frater (the first to be made,
a hoopoe, was inspired by a rare sighting of this bird in
the area in 2005; the other two sculptures are a barn
owl and a tern). Cross the **Howick Burn** by footbridge,
then continue along the track, with the low rock formations known as the Iron Scars on your R. After another

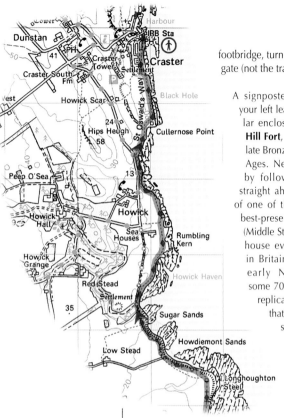

footbridge, turn R onto a path at the gate (not the track straight ahead).

A signposted footpath on your left leads to the circular enclosure of **Howick Hill Fort**, dating from the late Bronze and early Iron Ages. Nearby, accessed by following the track straight ahead, is the site of one of the earliest and best-preserved Mesolithic (Middle Stone Age) roundhouse ever to be found in Britain, inhabited by early Northumbrians some 7000 years ago. A replica of the circular, thatched hut can be seen here as well as at Milford, around 5 miles (8km) north of Wooler, where it forms part of the Maelmin Heritage Trail (www.maelmin.org.uk).

Shortly after this you pass a small sandy beach enclosed by rocks, not far from which is a sea arch (not very easy to spot from the trail) called **Rumbling Kern**, after the sound it makes. The low, angular sandstone cliffs at the S edge of the beach were a former quarry face. Immediately after this you pass a beautifully situated old stone house, originally a bathing house for the use of the second Earl Grey (of Earl Grey tea fame) and his family. The Grey family owned nearby Howick Hall – which, as

The bathing house built for the second Earl Grey, whose family owned Howick Hall, near Craster

it so happens, is where Earl Grey tea was first blended, to suit the water from the well there. ▶

Continue along a grit path, then around a grassy headland with more views of Dunstanburgh Castle ahead, and along a grassy path into **Craster**. This area, as well as that just to the N of Craster, are fine examples of Whin grassland, and will be particularly lush and flower-strewn in May. A little further along the road you come to the small, stout-walled **harbour**.

Howick Hall's beautiful gardens lie only around 1 mile (1.5km) inland from here, and can be visited February–November (**www. howickhallgardens. org**).

CRASTER

Just beyond the playground at the near end of Craster is the small 19th-century Church of St Peter. A little further along the road you will find the fish smokehouse for which the village is justly famous (L Robson & Sons, www. kipper.co.uk, tel: 01665 576223) – a large, mostly windowless, dark whinstone building with black tar from the smoking process literally oozing down the walls. The building has been here since 1865. There is a shop (where you can buy the delicious traditional oak-smoked kippers and salmon produced here) and a restaurant next to the smokehouse, and on the opposite side of the road the Jolly Fisherman pub (www.silk8234.fsnet.co.uk) is noted for its crab sandwiches and has an ATM. ▶

Round (rolled) hay bales in fields near Craster

Many of the houses in Craster are built of whinstone – you will notice they are darker than in most other towns and villages in the are – which is unusual, since it is a difficult stone to work, and therefore not particularly popular as a building material. A 15th-century round tower stands a short distance inland, near Dunstan. The harbour is a regular wintering spot for the Mediterranean gull.

Accommodation in Craster includes Harbour Lights B&B (www.harbourlights-craster.co.uk, tel: 01665 576062) and, around 10mins off-route in the villages of Dunstan, Stonecroft B&B (www.stonecroft-craster.co.uk, tel: 01665 576433). The bus stop for the 501 is near the playground (the stop serves both directions, as all buses turn round here).

STAGE 5
Craster to Bamburgh

Start	Harbour, Craster
Finish	The Green, Bamburgh
Distance	14 miles (22km)
Time	5hrs
Maps	OS Explorer 332 and 340; OS Landranger 75 and 81
Access	The 501 Berwick-upon-Tweed–Newcastle bus stops at Craster
Accommodation	Glenander B&B, Victoria Hotel and several alternatives in Bamburgh. At intermediate points, accommodation is available at Low Newton-by-the-Sea, Beadnell and Seahouses.

This is another easy day of walking along the coast, again with the option of walking along the beach itself at several points, passing the spectacular ruin of Dunstanburgh Castle and the beautifully preserved little fishing village of Low Newton-by-the-Sea.

Follow the road around **Craster**'s small fishing harbour, then continue along the coast on a grassy trail (another good example of Whin grassland, with a scattering of gorse) with the shattered walls and towers of Dunstanburgh Castle ahead of you, just off the main track.

Fishing boat beneath the massive walls of Craster harbour

The setting of **Dunstanburgh Castle** is magnificent. The castle occupies an elevated headland, and although the ruins are only fragmentary, it is still very clear this was a huge building. It is without any doubt one of the most atmospheric castles in the UK. Built in 1313 by the powerful Earl Thomas of Lancaster, at a time when

Map continues on page 92

relations between him and Edward II were deteriorating, it later passed to John of Gaunt, who strengthened it by converting the great twin-towered gatehouse into a keep. The headland is part of the Whin Sill, and the high whinstone cliffs on the northeast side of the headland are a favourite nesting place for seabirds, including kittiwakes and a small number of razorbills, which breed here in the summer months.

Return to the main trail and continue alongside Dunstanburgh Castle Golf Course. ▶ The trail cuts up onto the dunes, passing holiday homes, then descending alongside **Newton Pool Nature Reserve** (a good place to see migrant waterfowl and wading birds), where there are two hides. Join a road leading you around the back of the houses at **Low Newton-by-the-Sea**, a beautifully preserved 18th-century fishing village.

Low Newton-by-the-Sea consists of a pretty village green (Newton Square) surrounded on three sides

The ruins of Dunstanburgh Castle, on a headland just north of Craster

Depending on the tide, it is possible to walk along the beach of Embleton Bay into Low Newton, instead of following the dunes.

91

At low tide, you can walk along the beach itself from Newton Links, rejoining the main trail towards the N end of Beadnell Bay.

by white-painted cottages, overlooking Newton Haven. There is an excellent pub on the far side of the green, The Ship (www.shipinnnewton.co.uk, tel: 01665 576262), with wonderful food and real ales from its own highly acclaimed brewery, located just next door.

Continue following the trail along the coast, inland of Newton Point and passing the road end at **Newton Links**, then alongside the dunes of **Beadnell Bay**. ◄

Pass the low river flats and bends of the **Brunton Burn**, which you then cross by a wooden footbridge (known as Long Nanny Bridge). Walk through the large caravan park to reach the outskirts of **Beadnell** by Beadnell harbour. It is a walk of just under ½ mile (¾km) along the road to reach the other side of the village.

Beadnell harbour is the site of some exceptionally well-preserved late 18th-century limekilns, and on the headland east of the harbour are the scant remains of the 13th-

Map
continues on
page 94

century chapel of St Ebba. While the housing along the waterfront is modern and rather uninspiring, the older part of the village, which is reached by following The Haven left at the far end of the waterfront, is far more attractive. The church of St Ebba dates from the 18th century and has a Second World War memorial with stained glass by Joseph Edward Nuttgens, whose work includes some of the stained glass in Liverpool Cathedral. The Craster Arms (www.crasterarms.co.uk, tel: 01665 720272) offers food and accommodation, with the rear of the building formed by part of a medieval pele tower. The 501 bus stops just outside the Craster Arms.

Follow the coast N from Beadnell, with a view of Seahouses and the Farne Islands ahead. The route from here is mostly alongside the road (**B1340**), until ducking R across the golf course then L around the headland (and the sewage works) to arrive at the harbour and town centre of **Seahouses**.

Crossing the Brunton Burn near Beadnell

93

Seahouses

was only built
around the end of
the 19th century, after the harbour was established
to serve the booming herring trade and the local
lime industry (there is a group of old limekilns at
the harbour). While Seahouses is not the prettiest
of Northumberland's coastal towns, the harbour is
still a bustling little place, not least because it is the
departure point for boat trips to the Farne Islands.
There is a profusion of fish and chip shops around
the memorial at end of Main Street, as well as banks
and ATMs, and a decent-sized supermarket on

le Scarcar

↪ The Bush

Main Street as you walk towards North Sunderland. The 501 bus stops at the memorial.

Accommodation includes the Bamburgh Castle Inn (www.bamburghcastleinn. co.uk, tel: 01665 720283) and, just a further half a mile out of town on the route to Bamburgh and only 10mins off SOW, Springhill Farm (www. springhill-farm.co.uk, tel: 01665 721820).

FARNE ISLANDS

Located just offshore to the northeast of Seahouses, and managed as a nature reserve by the National Trust, the Farne Islands constitute the final outpost of the great Whin Sill. There are 28 islands in total, almost half of these disappearing at high tide; the largest is Inner Farne. St Aidan (founder of the monastery at Lindisfarne) occasionally spent time here, and St Cuthbert built a small cell on Inner Farne, where he died in 687. Benedictine monks from Durham followed in the 13th century, and St Cuthbert's Chapel was built in the 14th century, although it fell into ruin following the Dissolution, until renovated in the 19th century (including the addition of 17th-century furnishings from Durham Cathedral). The white lighthouse on Inner Farne dates from 1811 and was built by David Alexander – although there was a tower here as early as 1673. The red-and-white lighthouse on Longstone Rock, also by David Alexander, was built in 1826.

The islands are home to a spectacular concentration of birdlife, including puffins, eider ducks and several species of tern (the Arctic terns are fond of divebombing visitors, so wearing a hat is advisable to protect your scalp from attack!), with breeding colonies of guillemot, razorbill and kittiwake on the seastacks (the 'Pinnacles') of Staple Island, as well as some 3000–4000 grey seals. The best time of year to see birdlife is May–July, and the grey seals have their pups late October–November. Several companies run boat trips to the Farne Islands from Seahouses, including Billy Shiel's (the best-known and longest-running, www.farne-islands.com), Serenity (www.farneislandstours. co.uk) and Hanvey's (www.farne-islands.co.uk).

Depending on the tide, it is possible to walk N along the beach from Seahouses to Bamburgh instead of following the inland route described here. From the centre

The following day, rather than retracing your steps to North Sunderland, turn left in front of the farm to follow the road NE, to join up with SOW at North Cottage.

of Seahouses walk W along Main Street, passing restaurants and a supermarket, and following Osborne Terrace to the R shortly after the school, to reach the junction with Broad Road (alternatively if you have no need to stock up at the supermarket, a cycle track runs parallel to and just N of Main Street). If you are staying at Springhill Farm, cross Broad Road and continue along the road straight ahead. ◄

At the junction (where there is a rather impressive national cycle network sign), turn R onto Broad Road then L onto a footpath that takes you diagonally across the fields. On reaching the road at North Cottage turn R then immediately L down a quiet lane, as Bamburgh Castle comes into view. Turn R just before the caravan site at **Fowberry**, then roughly N over fields, passing by the houses at **Redbarns** (and crossing over several driveways), then over another field and L onto the road into **Bamburgh**. Follow the road along below the castle to the village green.

National cycle network sign near Seahouses

BAMBURGH

One of the finest castles anywhere in the UK, Bamburgh Castle (www.bamburghcastle.com) sits perched spectacularly on a high outcrop of the Whin Sill. There was a hill fort here as early as the Iron Age, and a fort and palace during the Anglo-Saxon period, when Bamburgh was the capital of Northumbria under King Oswald – although nothing of this remains. The keep dates from the 12th century, with the rest of the castle having been added to or rebuilt over the following centuries. In the 15th century Bamburgh had the distinction of being the first castle in England to be blown apart by cannon fire. It was bought by Lord Armstrong in the 19th century and renovated as a family home.

To the west of the green is St Aiden's church, dating from the 12th–13th century, probably on the site of an earlier wooden building built by St Aiden and King Oswald in the seventh century. It was heavily restored in the 19th century. In the churchyard there is a monument to local heroine Grace Darling – who along with her father, a lighthouse keeper at Longstone lighthouse, braved raging seas to rescue nine sailors from the wreck of the SS Forfarshire off the Farne Islands in 1838, while still in her early twenties. Opposite the church is the recently opened Grace Darling Museum (for more information including opening times, search for the museum on www.rnli.org.uk).

Accommodation in Bamburgh includes the Victoria Hotel (www.victoriahotel.net, tel: 01668 214431) and Glenander B&B (www.glenander.com, tel: 01668 214336). The 501 bus stops by The Grove, the triangular area of grass between St Aiden's and the green.

Below the ramparts of Bamburgh Castle

STAGE 6
Bamburgh to West Mains/Fenwick

Start	The Green, Bamburgh
Finish	Lindisfarne Inn, West Mains or Manor House B&B, Fenwick
Distance	14½ miles (23.5km) to West Mains; 13 miles (21km) to Fenwick
Time	7hrs (West Mains); 6hrs 35mins (Fenwick)
Maps	OS Explorer 340; OS Landranger 75
Access	The 501 Berwick-upon-Tweed–Newcastle bus stops at Bamburgh
Accommodation	The Lindisfarne Inn at West Mains has 21 rooms and good meals; Manor House B&B at Fenwick; limited options at Beal and, less conveniently, in West Kyloe. At intermediate points, accommodation is available at Belford.

North of Bamburgh, the route turns inland, crossing farmland and passing through the old market town of Belford and then Shiellow Wood. There is a brief section along the beach, followed by paths and forest tracks, with some road walking.

Most route descriptions list Bamburgh to Holy Island as one stage. However, for several reasons, it is better to break the journey before crossing to Holy Island itself, stopping for the night at either Fenwick, West Mains or Beal instead, before continuing the following day and spending a night on Holy Island. Firstly, to reach Holy Island you will need to cross the sands or the causeway at low tide – which may not coincide with your arrival. Secondly, it is a long stage from Bamburgh to Holy Island – 19 miles (31km); crossing during a morning or early afternoon low tide will allow you a more comfortable walk the day before. Finally, although there is quite a bit of accommodation available on Holy Island itself, it gets heavily booked, in particular during the summer, and some places require a minimum three-night stay, in which case West Mains, Beal and Fenwick can provide a welcome alternative.

If you are walking St Oswald's Way in the opposite direction to that described here (that is, from Holy Island to Heavenfield), reaching Bamburgh is only really feasible providing you can cross the sands or the causeway during an early morning low tide. It is still a long day, however.

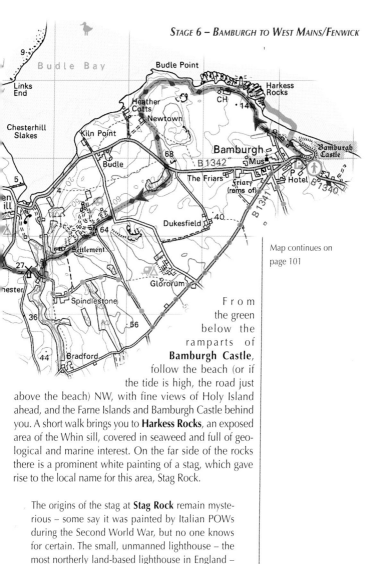

Map continues on
page 101

From
the green
below the
ramparts of
Bamburgh Castle,
follow the beach (or if
the tide is high, the road just
above the beach) NW, with fine views of Holy Island
ahead, and the Farne Islands and Bamburgh Castle behind
you. A short walk brings you to **Harkess Rocks**, an exposed
area of the Whin sill, covered in seaweed and full of geological and marine interest. On the far side of the rocks
there is a prominent white painting of a stag, which gave
rise to the local name for this area, Stag Rock.

The origins of the stag at **Stag Rock** remain myste-
rious – some say it was painted by Italian POWs
during the Second World War, but no one knows
for certain. The small, unmanned lighthouse – the
most northerly land-based lighthouse in England –
dates from 1910, although it was modernised in the
1970s.

Stag Rock

The path now veers L to the **golf club**, then descends R to the beach again, continuing along the beach or (depending on tides) on a grassy trail just above it, alongside the golf course. After rounding the headland you arrive at a ruined concrete pier (remarkably ugly given the setting). Turn L into the dunes, keeping L of the caravan park then veer R, ascending and passing old gun posts on your L.

Veer R, with the golf course on your L (and a hidden part of it on your R – watch out for golf balls!); go through a gate and onto the road, then L past **Newton Farm**. Keep straight ahead through a field, towards the hilltop, then follow the blue poles over another section of golf course, bearing R.

Turn L onto the road (confusingly, you are now walking straight back towards Bamburgh Castle), then turn R onto the road marked Dukesfield, and R again onto a path. Keeping the plantation on your R, skirt the side of the low hill, with Brada Quarry ahead and on your L, then alongside fields, with the path switching sides of the fence, and good views on your R.

Turn L onto a road, then R, and L again at **Waren Caravan Park**. Turn R onto a path alongside the caravans,

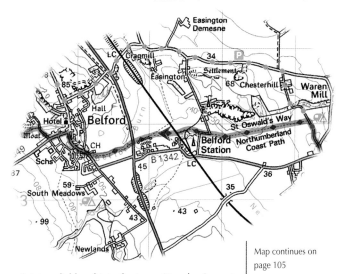

Map continues on page 105

veer L into a field and into the trees. At a clearing note the disused old limekiln on your L, and the rock forms of Spindlestone Heughs, an exposed section of the Whin Sill, rising above the trees behind you.

According to local legend, **Spindlestone Heughs** was a favourite perch of a dragon that caused much terror among the locals around Bamburgh Castle – although the dragon, we are told, was actually the daughter of the Anglo-Saxon King Ida, transformed into a 'laidly worm' by sorcery. Accordingly, the area just west of here is known as Laidly Worm's Trough. Spindlestone Heughs also has some fairly rare plant communities, which have earned it the status of SSSI.

Descend through woodland (slippery), then turn L onto a road. Follow this, crossing the bridge over the **Waren Burn**, and passing a converted **windmill** on your L.

Known as Spindlestone Ducket or Outchester Ducket, the **windmill** is often (wrongly) described as a dovecote, but would have once functioned as a threshing mill. It is one of only two such towers to have survived from threshing mills in Northumberland (www.rosscottages.co.uk).

Just north of here is the hamlet of Waren Mill (or Warren Mill), which had a corn mill as early as the 12th century and received a charter from Henry III in the 13th century. Once a busy port (for transporting corn, and lime from nearby kilns), its harbour has long since silted up with the sand and mud deposits of Budle Bay.

Take the road on your R, then turn R onto the main road (**B1342**), and L onto a minor road, before turning L onto a footpath signed for Belford. The path follows the line of the telegraph poles, with grain silos ahead (and on occasion the company of some rather over-inquisitive horses), before crossing a disused railway line (which leads to Easington Quarry, now closed).

Crossing the East Coast main railway line near Belford

Shortly after this you arrive at the East Coast **railway line**. Trains pass here at speeds in excess of 100mph, and

it is essential that you phone the signal box before crossing. Just use the telephone provided, confirm the number of people crossing, and the staff at the signal box will tell you whether it is safe to cross or not. Once you have been given the all clear, cross the tracks promptly. (You will need to repeat this process when crossing the railway line again, shortly before reaching the Holy Island causeway.)

The path now takes you past grain silos before crossing the **A1** (again, care is required here) and continuing over fields straight ahead. After skirting a golf driving range, arrive at **Belford Golf Club**, then turn R along the road to the market square and cross in **Belford**.

> **Belford** is an old market town, which lay on the Great North Road. St Mary's Church, just north of the market square, includes a chancel arch dating from the Norman period, and stained-glass windows by CE Kempe (whose other work includes Bristol Cathedral). There is an 18th-century cross in the market square, and the 18th-century Belford Hall lies just to the northeast of the village.
>
> Accommodation includes the Blue Bell Hotel (www.bluebellhotel.com, tel: 01668 213543), an old coaching inn, and The Old Vicarage B&B (www. belfordoldvicarage.co.uk, tel: 01668 213025). There is a supermarket and a lovely wooden toy shop (although this might not be what you feel like carrying for another three days!). The 501 and 505 bus services stop in Belford.

Turn L from the square, passing a supermarket on your L, then take a road on your R (no footpath sign or waymarking), then a path on your L. Turn R onto a grass track, with **Westhall** (a fortified 19th-century house in Gothic style) on your R. Beyond Westhall is Chapel Crag, another outcrop of the Whin Sill, and once the site of a medieval chapel. Flints tools dating back to the Mesolithic period have also been found at Chapel Crag.

Pass a small area of woodland on your L (a spot known, rather charmingly, as The Hag – which actually means in local dialect a ridge of exposed peat), but do not take the path to the L immediately after this. The route is rather unclear here, but the trick is to keep straight ahead and L, just below the ridge, with the fence on your L (do not descend R towards the gate), aiming slightly L of the gap between the two woods ahead.

Turn L through the stile, then keep straight ahead through the buildings of **Swinhoe Farm** (where it is thought that some of Cromwell's soldiers took refuge in a barn during the English Civil War), and follow the track straight ahead after these (not R or L). Pass **Swinhoe Lake** on your R (keep an eye out for birdlife here, and for deer in the surrounding fields), then emerge from Virgin Hill Wood through a gate. Continue with Fawcett Hill on your R, and views of Greensheen Hill ahead on your L. Just to the S of Greensheen Hill is an area of woodland, **St Cuthbert's Cave Woods**. At the time of writing the whole area on your L between Fawcett Hill and St Cuthbert's Cave Wood is the proposed site of a large windfarm – see the St Cuthbert's Way route description for more details.

You soon arrive at a stile at the junction of St Oswald's Way and St Cuthbert's Way – the trail markings of SCW

Livestock shelter on the side of Fawcett Hill

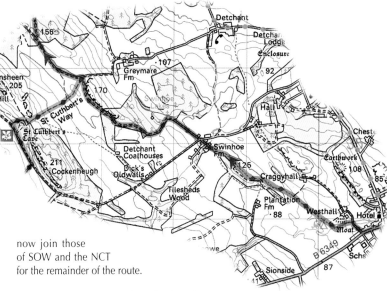

now join those
of SOW and the NCT
for the remainder of the route.

Map continues on
page 106

St Cuthbert's Cave is believed to have been a resting place for the body of the seventh-century saint, carried by the monks of Lindisfarne when they left Holy Island in the face of repeated Viking raids. It can easily be visited as a short and very worthwhile detour from the main route. Follow the SCW trail markings southwest across fields from the junction of SOW and SCW, over a shoulder and down alongside St Cuthbert's Cave Wood. Turn left onto a track into the wood, to reach a clear path up to the cave on your left. Allow 25mins each way.

Below the north slopes of Greensheen Hill is **Holburn Lake and Moss**. The lake is an important wintering site for greylag geese, which arrive here from Iceland, and the surrounding peat mire is one of the few such intact areas of raised peat mire in the UK. Holburn Lake and Moss, along with Greensheen Hill, are Special Protected Areas (SPAs), and Holburn Lake is a RAMSAR site. The lake is actually manmade and was only created in 1934.

Those following the route description for St Cuthbert's Way should start here.

◄ From the stile at the junction of the trails, turn L onto a track, with views of Holy Island on your R, to arrive at **Shiellow Wood**. After entering the wood, take the signposted track on your R, pass another track and then Shiellow Crag House, both on your R. Keep straight ahead, crossing a stream by way of a small bridge, then cross a track, keeping straight ahead on a path signposted to Fenwick. Cross a

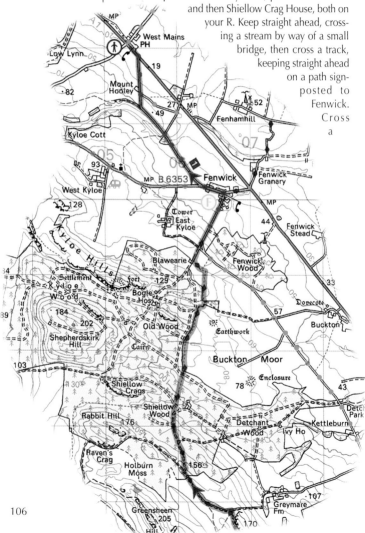

series of small wooden bridges and streams, with clear waymarkings, to reach a stile at the edge of the wood. Continue alongside fields, following the course of what was once an old lane known as Dolly Gibson's Lonnen.

Lindisfarne Castle on Holy Island, and the navigation posts at Ross Point, viewed from above Detchant, just off SOW

> The woods on your left, **Kyloe Woods**, are an important reserve for the red squirrel, and it was here that some of the first leylandii cypress stock – now a popular hybrid hedging shrub – was grown in the 19th century.

Veer L to arrive at a farm, before turning R and following the road (once part of the Great North Road) downhill to the small settlement of **Fenwick**.

Those staying at the Lindisfarne Inn (www.lindisfarne inn.co.uk, tel: 01289 381223) in **West Mains** should turn L along the B6353 from Fenwick (towards West Kyloe), then R onto a minor road that leads past Mount Hooly and joins the A1 just a short distance from the inn (allow 25mins). For Beal, either follow the road towards Holy Island from West Mains (15mins), or follow the route description from Fenwick towards Holy Island, turning L onto the road just before the causeway. Fenwick's only accommodation is Manor House B&B (www.manorhouse fenwick.co.uk, tel: 01289 381016), so the chances are most walkers will need to stay at West Mains. The 501 and 505 buses stop outside the Lindisfarne Inn, West Mains.

STAGE 7
West Mains/Fenwick to Holy Island

Start	Lindisfarne Inn, West Mains or Manor House B&B, Fenwick
Finish	Lindisfarne Priory, Holy Island
Distance	7½ miles (12km) from West Mains; 6 miles (9.5km) from Fenwick
Time	2hrs 45mins from West Mains; 2hrs 20mins from Fenwick. (Timings include 1hr to cross the sands.)
Maps	OS Explorer 340; OS Landranger 75
Access	501 and 505 buses to Fenwick
Accommodation	Either a second night at the Lindisfarne Inn in West Mains if visiting Holy Island as a day trip; or the Crown and Anchor on Holy Island itself; several other options on Holy Island.
Note	For the final part of the route across the sands to Holy Island you must observe the safe crossing times. Go to www.northumberland.gov.uk and click on *Leisure, Tourism & Culture* followed by *Holy Island Tide Times*.

A short and very easy stage, this follows the 'Pilgrim's Way' across the sands to Holy Island. If you have stayed at West Mains, retrace your steps to Fenwick. Alternatively, a more direct option is to simply head down the road past Beal – there is a cycle track beside the road – to rejoin the main route at the causeway.

Even if you do not plan to stay on Holy Island and intend to visit as a 'day trip' (for example, between two nights at West Mains), you must still time your return to coincide with safe crossing times.

Continue through **Fenwick** on the B6353, cross the A1 and continue on the road straight ahead, past **Fenwick Granary**. Veer R past the farm, crossing a cattle grid, then turn L onto a path and ascend, passing a disused quarry. Turn R onto a road then L along a track known as Fishers Back Road.

A little under 1½ miles (2km) from Fenwick you cross the East Coast **railway line** again. As before, it is essential that you call the signal box before crossing, using the phone provided, to check whether there are any trains

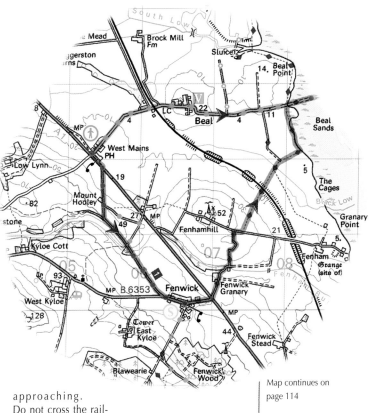

Map continues on page 114

approaching.
Do not cross the rail-
way lines before you have been given the all clear.

Head down through the caravan site, and follow the track straight ahead, before turning R onto a path and then L along the coast to the **Holy Island causeway**. ▶

After confirming the safe crossing times at the entrance to the Holy Island causeway, follow the road for a short distance, crossing the bridge over South Low to the first refuge box. It takes at least 1hr for the 2½ mile (4.5km) crossing over the sands – some even advise allowing up to 2hrs if the sand is soft – and you can only cross them safely during the middle of the safe crossing period. Ideally, you should aim to *complete* your crossing by the midpoint of the safe crossing period.

Beal, just 1 mile (1.5km) up the road to the W, takes its name from 'bee hill', and is thought to have supplied honey to Holy Island.

Following the Pilgrim's Route across the sands to Holy Island

The OS maps have the route of SOW marked along the causeway, but instead strike out ESE across the sands along the Pilgrim's Route, following the clear line of the marker poles. Water generally lies in patches across the sands even at low tide, so crossing barefoot may be preferable, or in sandals or wellies. Note the refuge box atop one of the marker poles – people do still get stranded crossing to Holy Island, both on the sands and the causeway, although there is no reason to do so providing you observe the safe crossing times. As you walk, keep an eye out for waterfowl, of which these vast tidal flats has plenty. You might also reflect how this beautiful tidal area was used for bombing practice during the Second World War.

Approximately 1hr after leaving the road by South Low, you arrive at **Chare Ends** on Holy Island (Lindisfarne). Follow the road straight ahead and around to the R, passing the substantial car park and striding into the small village of **Holy Island**.

HOLY ISLAND

The 'rainbow arch' at the ruins of Lindisfarne Priory. This rib from the priory's vault survived the collapse of the surrounding roof and tower above it

The Irish monk St Aidan founded a **priory** on Holy Island (Lindisfarne) in AD635, at the request of the Anglo-Saxon King Oswald. Holy Island was to become one of the most important early centres of Christianity in England, responsible for producing the beautiful Lindisfarne Gospels in the early 700s. Nothing remains of the first monastery, which was destroyed by Viking raids in the late eighth and ninth centuries, with the monks themselves departing in 875. In 1083 the monastery was refounded by the Bishop of Durham, and the rather magnificent red sandstone ruin seen today dates from between this time and the first half of the 12th century, with the monastic buildings added in the 13th century and later.

Directly opposite the entrance to the priory is **St Mary's Church**, the oldest church on Holy Island. Much of the building dates from the 13th century, but some elements of an earlier building are still visible – including some Saxon details. The church was restored in the 19th century, and has stained glass by Franz Mayer.

Just to the south of the priory is a small knoll known as the Heugh, where there was once a small fort. The memorial cross is by Edwin Lutyens, the architect responsible for renovating Lindisfarne Castle in the early 1900s. The Heugh is part of the Holy Island Dyke, an outcrop of the Whin Sill, upon which the castle is also built. The views are excellent – note the ▶

Cairns above the beach at Castle Point

navigation posts on Ross Sands, over on the mainland. A short distance offshore, to the west of the priory and the Heugh, is a small island, where St Cuthbert once had a monastic cell, and the remains of a medieval chapel can still be seen. Elsewhere in the village you will find the Lindisfarne Centre (www.lindisfarne-centre.com), with exhibitions and a shop, the St Cuthbert Centre (www.holyisland-stcuthbert.org), and St Aiden's Winery (www.lindisfarne-mead.co.uk), home of the well-known local mead. The village cross in the market square dates from 1828.

The ancient sand dune systems of Holy Island are rich in flowers and grasses, supporting species such as coral-root orchid and the endemic Lindisfarne helleborine.

West of the castle at Castle Point is a well-preserved group of limekilns (for a good appreciation of how they would have looked when working, see the large oil painting by John Moore from 1877 in the entrance hall of the castle, which depicts the castle and priory with the limekilns burning in the moonlight). Above the east shore of Holy Island, just beyond the castle and the limekilns, you will often find carefully arranged cairns and piles of stones, and sometimes more elaborate creations – on one visit I saw a beautifully observed horse in small black and white stones – left by visitors and pilgrims. Beyond, the grey expanse of the North Sea stretches to the horizon. Just to the north of the castle is the small walled garden designed and laid out by Gertrude Jekyll in 1911, for Edward Hudson.

Accommodation on Holy Island includes the Crown & Anchor (www.holyislandcrown.co.uk, tel: 01289 389215), the Lindisfarne Hotel (www.thelindisfarnehotel.co.uk, tel: 01289 389273) and Bamburgh View B&B (tel: 01289 389212).

Walks around Holy Island

There are several short walks that allow you to explore Holy Island further. The first, and most obvious, is to continue E from the priory then N from **Lindisfarne Castle**, following the coast and completing a circuit of the island (3 miles (5km), allow 1½hrs). As you walk around the harbour (known as the Ouse) from the priory to reach the castle, note the upturned fishing boats, the hulls of which have been sawn in half and converted into small sheds.

> **Lindisfarne Castle**, which was built in 1549–50, was bought by Edward Hudson (founder of *Country Life* magazine) in 1901, and transformed into a home by architect Edwin Lutyens. It occupies a spectacular position on a steep outcrop of the Whin Sill, and its interior is a fascinating warren of passages and vaulted rooms. The castle provided a suitably atmospheric setting for Roman Polanski's 1966 film *Cul-de-Sac*.

On the eastern side of the island you pass the Lough, a shallow freshwater lake (perhaps established by the

The ruins of Lindisfarne Priory, Holy Island

113

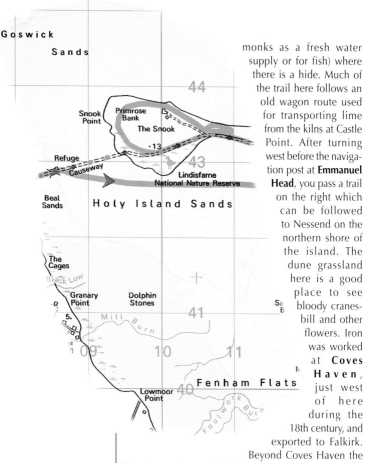

monks as a fresh water supply or for fish) where there is a hide. Much of the trail here follows an old wagon route used for transporting lime from the kilns at Castle Point. After turning west before the navigation post at **Emmanuel Head**, you pass a trail on the right which can be followed to Nessend on the northern shore of the island. The dune grassland here is a good place to see bloody cranesbill and other flowers. Iron was worked at **Coves Haven**, just west of here during the 18th century, and exported to Falkirk. Beyond Coves Haven the limestone outcrop of **Back Skerrs** projects out into the sea. Return to the main route, then turn south, passing old limekilns and return to the car park.

Another option is to follow a shorter circuit around the **Snook** – an old dune system, and once the focus of coal mining activity – starting and finishing at a parking area part way back along the road to the causeway (2 miles (3.5km), allow 1hr). Alternatively, from the same start/finish point, you can explore The Big Bank (1½ miles

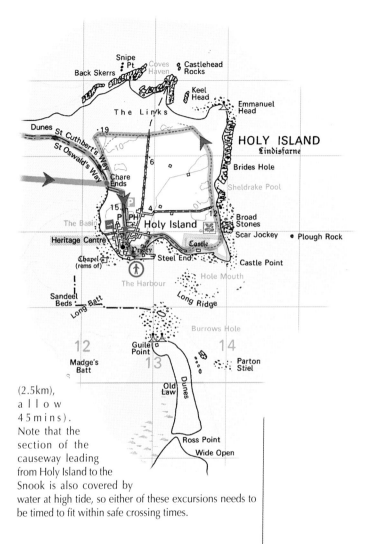

(2.5km),
a l l o w
4 5 m i n s).
Note that the
section of the
causeway leading
from Holy Island to the
Snook is also covered by
water at high tide, so either of these excursions needs to
be timed to fit within safe crossing times.

STAGE 8

Holy Island to Berwick-upon-Tweed

Start	Lindisfarne Priory, Holy Island
Finish	Railway station, Berwick-upon-Tweed
Distance	13 miles (20.5km)
Time	5hrs 30mins (including 1hr to cross the sands)
Maps	OS Explorer 340, 341 and 346; OS Landranger 75
Access	The 501 and 505 Berwick-upon-Tweed–Newcastle bus and the 477 Berwick-upon-Tweed–Holy Island (Wed and Sat) stop at Beal/Holy Island road end. From the finish at Berwick-upon-Tweed East Coast Trains run to destinations including London, Edinburgh and Newcastle.
Accommodation	For those wishing to break this into two stages, there is East House B&B near Cheswick Sands; plenty of choice of accommodation in Berwick-upon-Tweed itself, including the 1 Sallyport Hotel.
Note	There is a possible danger of **unexploded ordnance** around Goswick Sands and the dunes behind Cheswck Sands. Pay attention to warning signs.

This is an easy day with some road walking – much of which can be avoided by following the coast itself, including Goswick and Cheswick Sands – and some of the finest coastal scenery anywhere in the UK. If you have stayed at West Mains instead of on Holy Island, follow the road down to the causeway (2 miles or 3km), and pick up the route there.

From **Holy Island**, follow the Pilgrim's Route across the sands at low tide (allow at least 1hr). From the car park just inland from the causeway, follow the NCP sign and head N along the coast, passing initially between a double row of concrete anti-tank blocks from the Second World War, and then passing a pair of World War II pillboxes on your left. The path here is apt to be marshy and the tide can reach quite high, in which case there are sections of path higher up on the bank on the left if necessary.

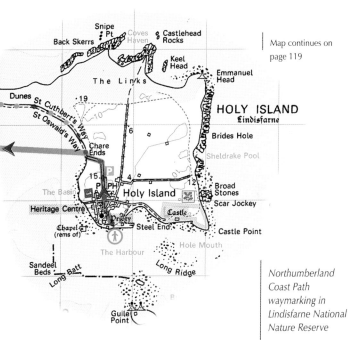

Map continues on page 119

Snipe Pt
Back Skerrs
Coves Haven
Castlehead Rocks
Keel Head
Emmanuel Head
The Links
Dunes
St Cuthbert's Way
St Oswald's Way
19
10
HOLY ISLAND
Lindisfarne
6
Brides Hole
Chare Ends
Sheldrake Pool
15.
P
4
12
Broad Stones
P PH
Scar Jockey
The Basin
Holy Island
Heritage Centre
Priory
Castle
Broad Stones
Chapel (rems of)
Steel End
Castle Point
The Harbour
Hole Mouth
Sandeel Beds
Long Ridge
Long Batt
B
Guile Point

Northumberland Coast Path waymarking in Lindisfarne National Nature Reserve

117

After reaching a perpendicular track, turn R onto this and cross above the **sluice gates** over South Low. The path bends round to the R then L again, heading for the buildings of **Beachcomber House** (a campsite here closed in 2011) and the ruins of a World War II observation tower.

Map continues on page 121

Goswick Sands was used for live bombing practice during the Second World War (hence the observation tower), and there is still a possible danger

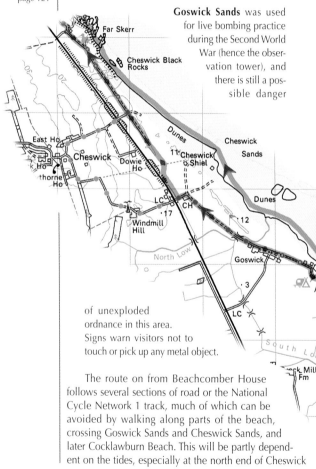

of unexploded ordnance in this area. Signs warn visitors not to touch or pick up any metal object.

The route on from Beachcomber House follows several sections of road or the National Cycle Network 1 track, much of which can be avoided by walking along parts of the beach, crossing Goswick Sands and Cheswick Sands, and later Cocklawburn Beach. This will be partly dependent on the tides, especially at the north end of Cheswick

Sands, around the rocks of Far Skerr – and read the signs warning of the potential danger of live ordnance on Goswick Sands. Check the Lindisfarne safe crossing times for an indication of the tides here. In any case, there are several points at which you can cross from the beach to the road or track, as marked on the map. Walking times will be similar either way.

From the former campsite, continue straight ahead on the road, passing yet another golf course on your right (this is the last one), and turning L on the road after the **clubhouse**. Do not cross the East Coast main line but instead take the path on your R just before the railway crossing, alongside the golf practice range, then R at the end of this, and L onto an embankment alongside the N end of the golf course.

Around 4 miles (6.5km) from the Holy Island causeway you reach a road end and National Cycle Network 1. Whether or not you intend to follow the beach, take the path to the R here which leads up onto the dunes and down onto the broad sweep of **Cheswick Sands**, for a view of what is surely one of the most beautiful stretches of coastline anywhere in the UK. The dunes here are some of the highest of the Northumberland coast. (Caution: the fenced area behind and inland from the dunes was once an old military firing range, and signs warn

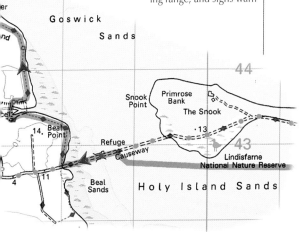

Cheswick Sands, site of some of the tallest sand dunes on the Northumberland coast, looking S to Goswick Sands

Turning L onto the road here will take you to East House B&B (**www.easthousebed andbreakfast.co.uk**) – an exceptionally lovely place to stay, just 10mins' walk from the dunes of Cheswick Sands.

not to walk in this area due to the danger of unexploded ordnance.) ◀

To follow the road rather than the beach, retrace your steps and and go along the cycle route, passing a pond on your L (a former limestone quarry), and footpaths down to the beach and **Cocklawburn Dunes Nature Reserve** and Middle and Far Skerrs on your R.

The Skerrs here are exposed sections of folded limestone projecting into the sea, and are particularly rich in fossils. You will also find the ruins of an old limekiln near Middle Skerr, a further reminder of the former importance of this industry in the area (as well as limestone, sandstone was also quarried locally, and there was an important coal mine just inland from here at Scremerston).

Pass a prominent World War II gun turret on your R, followed by a small car park and a path down to **Cocklawburn Beach**. Saltpan Rocks just to the N of here was once the site of a small salt making industry, where seawater was evaporated in large pans heated by coal. Continue past

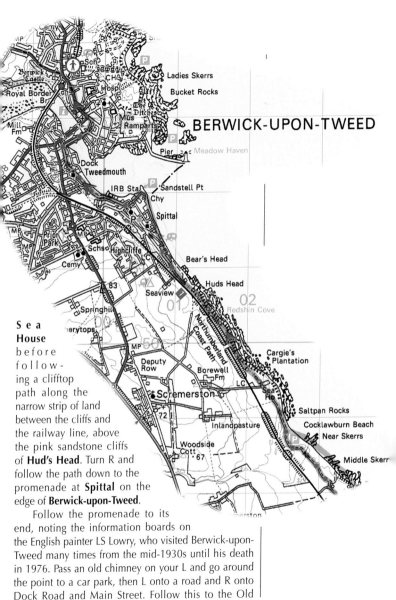

Sea House before following a clifftop path along the narrow strip of land between the cliffs and the railway line, above the pink sandstone cliffs of **Hud's Head**. Turn R and follow the path down to the promenade at **Spittal** on the edge of **Berwick-upon-Tweed**.

Follow the promenade to its end, noting the information boards on the English painter LS Lowry, who visited Berwick-upon-Tweed many times from the mid-1930s until his death in 1976. Pass an old chimney on your L and go around the point to a car park, then L onto a road and R onto Dock Road and Main Street. Follow this to the Old

W Cowe & Sons, the Original Berwick Cockle Shop, which opened on Bridge Street in 1886, closed its doors in 2010

Bridge, completed in 1626, with views of the impressive Elizabethan walls on the other side of the Tweed.

To reach the railway station, cross the bridge (note the sundial on the R at the far end) and either walk straight ahead up West Street then L onto Marygate and straight ahead along Castlegate; or turn L after the Old Bridge alongside the river, under the Royal Tweed Bridge, then R up a path and flights of steps just before Berwick's famous railway bridge, the Royal Border Bridge (either way, it is about an hour's walk from the promenade in Spittal to the station).

BERWICK-UPON-TWEED

Berwick-upon-Tweed, with its trio of bridges spanning the River Tweed, has an old town centre encircled by one of the most complete sections of Elizabethan fortifications anywhere in Britain. Passed repeatedly back and forth between English and Scottish hands – it has been English since 1482 – Berwick was sacked more than a dozen times between the 11th and 15th centuries. The medieval walls were begun by Edward I in 1296. However, these were not sufficient protection against artillery and in 1558 an elaborate, Italianate system of bastions was designed by Richard Lee (previously responsible for the defences at Portsmouth). The Old Bridge was completed in 1626. The Royal Border Bridge, 1847–50, soars across the Tweed like a Roman aqueduct, its 28 arches carrying the East Coast railway line into Berwick station at a height of 38.5m. Between the two is the concrete Royal Tweed Bridge, built in the 1920s.

The Church of the Holy Trinity was built in the 1650s, with some restoration in the 19th century. In the south aisle is a monument to Colonel Fenwicke, who commissioned the church. The windows include 16th–17th-century Dutch and Flemish stained glass. Berwick Castle – which stood at one corner of the older, medieval walls – was demolished in the 19th century to make way for the railway station, which stands on the site of the Great Hall. There is a Lowry Trail (www.berwick-pt.co.uk/lowry_trail.htm), which visits many of the places in Berwick painted by LS Lowry.

Accommodation in Berwick-upon-Tweed includes the 1 Sallyport Hotel (www.sallyport.co.uk, tel: 01289 308827).

The Old Bridge in Berwick-upon-Tweed, built in 1611

NORTHUMBERLAND COAST PATH

The Northumberland Coast Path stretches from Cresswell to Berwick-upon-Tweed, a distance of 64 miles (103km), which includes the entire length of the Northumberland Coast AONB, as well as Druridge Bay to the south. It can be comfortably covered in 5–6 days.

With the exception of the initial 10 miles or so (16km) between Cresswell and Warkworth, its route follows that of St Oswald's Way from Warkworth to Berwick-upon-Tweed (SOW Stages 4–8) – in which case, if combined with the breakdown of stages for St Oswald's Way (and including a visit to Holy Island), the stages would be as follows:

- **Stage 1** Cresswell to Warkworth – 10½ miles (16.5km)
- **Stage 2** Warkworth to Craster – 13½ miles (21.5km)
- **Stage 3** Craster to Bamburgh – 14 miles (22km)
- **Stage 4** Bamburgh to West Mains/Fenwick – 14½ miles (23.5km)/13 miles (21km)
- **Stage 5** West Mains/Fenwick to Holy Island – 6 miles (9.5km)
- **Stage 6** Holy Island to Berwick-upon-Tweed – 13 miles (20.5km)

For walkers who want to be sure of completing the Northumberland Coast Path, its first stage is outlined below.

The Northumberland Coast Path constitutes just one section of the North Sea Trail – a mammoth route including sections of the Norwegian, Swedish, Danish, Dutch, German and UK coasts around the North Sea basin. For more information see www.northseatrail.org.

The abbreviation NCP has been used for the Northumberland Coast Path throughout the route description, and NST for the North Sea Trail.

STAGE 1
Cresswell to Warkworth

Start	Steps to beach, Cresswell
Finish	Market square, Warkworth
Distance	10½ miles (16.5km)
Time	3hrs 30mins
Maps	OS Explorer 335 and 332; OS Landranger 81
Access	East Coast Trains to Newcastle, followed by the X20, X21 or X22 bus from Newcastle to Ashington, and the number 1 bus from Ashington to Cresswell. The 518 bus between Newcastle and Alnwick stops in Amble and Warkworth.
Accommodation	Warkworth House Hotel; if stopping in Amble, Harbour Guesthouse B&B.

The first stage follows the coast around Druridge Bay to Amble and historic Warkworth. It gives an easy mixture of beach walking, paths and tracks, with a short section of road walking.

▶ From **Cresswell**, with its 12th-century pele tower set back just SW and inland from the village, follow the beach N, first along the sands of **Druridge Bay** then after just over 2 miles (3.5km), along a track behind the dunes, passing Druridge Pools.

Just inland from here are the ruins of **Chibburn Preceptory** (Preceptory of St John o f

Cresswell Pond Nature Reserve, an excellent spot for watching waders and waterfowl (and the occasional exotic migrant) and a SSSI, is just inland across the coast road.

Map continues on page 126

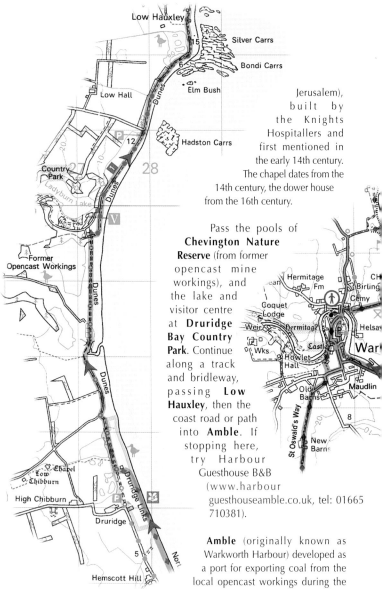

Jerusalem), built by the Knights Hospitallers and first mentioned in the early 14th century. The chapel dates from the 14th century, the dower house from the 16th century.

Pass the pools of **Chevington Nature Reserve** (from former opencast mine workings), and the lake and visitor centre at **Druridge Bay Country Park**. Continue along a track and bridleway, passing **Low Hauxley**, then the coast road or path into **Amble**. If stopping here, try Harbour Guesthouse B&B (www.harbour guesthouseamble.co.uk, tel: 01665 710381).

Amble (originally known as Warkworth Harbour) developed as a port for exporting coal from the local opencast workings during the

19th century. Coquet Island, an RSPB reserve and a SSSI, is famous for its birdlife including puffins and roseate terns. Boat trips run from Amble during the summer (landing on the island itself is prohibited).

Follow the S shore of the Coquet Estuary into **Warkworth**, where accommodation

Redshank at Cresswell Pond, a short detour from the Northumberland Coast Path

05

North Steel

Coquet Island
NORTHUMBERLAND

South Steel

Warkworth Harbour

LB Sta

Marina

Pan Point

Cemy

Wellhaugh Point

AMBLE

Activity Centre

Dunes

High Hauxley

Low Hauxley

Hauxley Haven

Warkworth Castle includes the Warkworth House Hotel (www.warkworth househotel.co.uk, tel: 01665 711276), near the old bridge.

To continue
To complete the Northumberland Coast Path follow St Oswald's Way Stages 4–8.

ST CUTHBERT'S WAY

Trail leading up to the border ridge in the Cheviot hills, where St Cuthbert's Way crosses from the Borders into Northumberland (Stage 3)

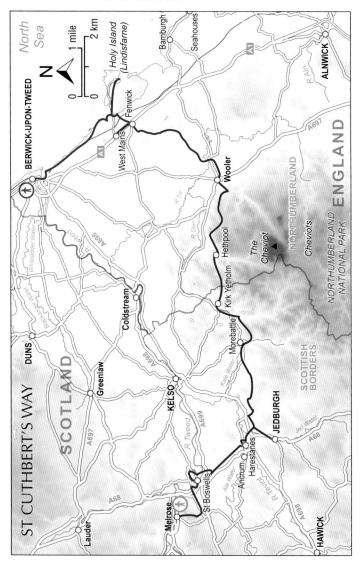

INTRODUCTION

Boot scraper in woods near Monteviot House (Stage 2)

St Cuthbert's Way was opened in 1996, its route covering a distance of 62 miles (100km) from Melrose, in the Borders, to Holy Island (Lindisfarne) on the north Northumberland coast. The route links several sites associated with the life of the seventh-century St Cuthbert: Melrose Abbey, of which St Cuthbert was prior; St Cuthbert's Cave, where monks fleeing from Lindisfarne carrying the saint's body and other relics stopped to rest; and Holy Island itself, where St Cuthbert was prior and later bishop. The walk, which is divided roughly equally between the Borders and Northumberland, visits three of the great Border abbeys and several unspoilt villages, before crossing the Cheviots and winding through more history-studded landscape to the Northumberland Coast.

In this guide there are a few slight changes to the standard breakdown of stages of St Cuthbert's Way. Firstly, in the conventional route, the first stage finishes at Harestanes, but there is no accommodation here – necessitating a detour to nearby Ancrum or Jedburgh. For this reason, in this guide the first stage has been extended into Jedburgh (which has far more accommodation available than Ancrum, and gives walkers a chance to visit the magnificent Jedburgh Abbey) along a section of the Border Abbeys Way. Secondly, the short detour to

Dryburgh Abbey is here treated as an integral part of the route. Third and finally, as with St Oswald's Way, walkers are advised to consider stopping at Fenwick or West Mains rather than walking from Wooler to Holy Island in one day, since crossing to Holy Island is dependent on tides and safe crossing times, and is thus not always possible in the evening (see Hill and coastal safety).

The standard route description for St Cuthbert's Way is usually spread over four days, and it shares some of its route in Scotland with the Border Abbeys Way and the Pennine Way, and some of its final stages in Northumberland with St Oswald's Way and the Northumberland Coast Path.

For reference, the 'standard' Melrose–Holy Island route is usually described as:

- **Stage 1** Melrose to Harestanes – 15 miles (24km)
- **Stage 2** Harestanes to Kirk Yetholm – 16½ miles (27km)
- **Stage 3** Kirk Yetholm to Wooler – 13 miles (21km)
- **Stage 4** Wooler to Holy Island – 16½ miles (27km)

In this guide, as with St Oswald's Way, the route is described as continuing from Holy Island up the coast to Berwick-upon-Tweed – an additional 13 miles (20.5km) – following the Northumberland Coast Path. This avoids a walk back along the road to West Mains, and allows walkers to take advantage of the better

transport links from Berwick. Just as importantly, the extended walk passes through some of the most beautiful coastal scenery in Britain. This increases the length of the route to 79 miles (127km), which would best be spread over six days.

A summary of the stages described here is as follows:

- **Stage 1** Melrose to Jedburgh – 19½ miles (32km)
- **Stage 2** Jedburgh to Kirk Yetholm – 16 miles (26km)
- **Stage 3** Kirk Yetholm to Wooler – 13 miles (21km)
- **Stage 4** Wooler to West Mains/Fenwick – 13 miles (21.5km)/11½ miles (19km)
- **Stage 5** West Mains/Fenwick to Holy Island – 6 miles (9.5km)
- **Stage 6** Holy Island to Berwick-upon-Tweed – 13 miles (20.5km)

For those who want to follow the route at a more leisurely pace, the following breakdown of stages is recommended:

- **Stage 1** Melrose to St Boswell's – 7½ miles (12km)
- **Stage 2** St Boswell's to Jedburgh – 12 miles (19.5km)
- **Stage 3** Jedburgh to Morebattle – 9½ miles (15km)
- **Stage 4** Morebattle to Kirk Yetholm – 6½ miles (11km)
- **Stage 5** Kirk Yetholm to Hethpool – 5 miles (8km)
- **Stage 6** Hethpool to Wooler – 8 miles (13km)

View over the River Tweed to the Eildon Hills, from near Dryburgh Abbey (Stage 1)

- **Stage 7** Wooler to West Mains/Fenwick – 13 miles (21.5km)/11½ miles (19km)
- **Stage 8** West Mains/Fenwick to Holy Island – 6 miles (9.5km)
- **Stage 9** Holy Island to Berwick-upon-Tweed – 13 miles (20.5km)

There is plenty of accommodation in Jedburgh and Wooler, slightly less at Kirk Yetholm. As mentioned previously, there is no accommodation at Harestanes. There is only one B&B at Fenwick so most walkers will find it more convenient to stop at West Mains – which also has the advantage of being slightly closer to Holy Island, for those intending to visit as a day trip. There are also several places to stay at intermediate points on the route, including St Boswell's.

STAGE 1
Melrose to Jedburgh

Start	Melrose Abbey, Melrose
Finish	Jedburgh Abbey, Jedburgh
Distance	19½ miles (32km)
Time	8hrs 15mins
Maps	OS Explorer 338 and OL16; OS Landranger 73
Access	East Coast Trains to Berwick-upon-Tweed, followed by bus (number 67) to Melrose. There is also a bus service from Edinburgh (62).
Accommodation	Glenbank House Hotel and several alternatives in Jedburgh. Accommodation also available in St Boswells and (more limited) in Ancrum.

This is an easy – although long – stage that takes in a wealth of historical and scenic interest, including the abbeys at Melrose, Dryburgh and Jedburgh, Roman Dere Street, the Eildon Hills and the River Tweed. There are good paths with some road walking, and a short, steep climb over the Eildons. If preferred, this stage can conveniently be broken into two stages by stopping at St Boswells.

The route description and timings include a visit to the superbly atmospheric Dryburgh Abbey, just off the main route of SCW before St Boswells.

This first stage is usually described as finishing at Harestanes; however, as there is no accommodation there this effectively means a detour to Ancrum, a 1-mile (1.5km) road walk (but accommodation there is very limited), or continuiing to Jedburgh, as described here. Alternatively you could take a bus (number 68) from Ancrum to Jedburgh, and return by bus in the morning.

From **Melrose Abbey**, follow the road S to the market square, then straight ahead up Dingleton Road and under the flyover carrying the A68. Turn L down a flight of steps signposted Eildon Walk and SCW, then ascend a steep path (which can be slippery after rain) with occasional sections of steps. Veer R to gain a saddle (320m) between the two main **Eildon Hills**.

MELROSE

The Church of St Mary the Virgin at Melrose Abbey (search for 'Melrose Abbey' on www.historic-scotland.gov.uk) was founded in 1136, although much of it dates from the late 14th century, after it was largely destroyed by an army led by Richard II in 1385. It is a magnificent building, rich in sculptural detail, from saints to gargoyles, courtiers and demons – look out for the bagpipe-playing pig on the south exterior walls of the church. The church is thought to be the burial place of Robert the Bruce's heart, and is also the final resting place of the Scottish King Alexander II. It is worth climbing the stairs to the rooftop, both for the view of the abbey itself, and of the Eildon Hills to the south, which our route crosses after leaving Melrose.

Old Melrose, thought to have been the site of the monastery during St Cuthbert's lifetime, lies about 2½ miles (4km) east of town. The site of Trimontium, a large Roman military camp, lies just east of Melrose at Newstead, and there is a small museum in the Ormiston Institute on the main square in Melrose itself (www.trimontium.org.uk). According to legend, King Arthur lies buried somewhere in the nearby Eildon Hills – although there is of course no evidence for this. Along the minor road leading southeast from Melrose over the flanks of the Eildons is the Rhymer's Stone, a memorial to the 13th-century Thomas the Rhymer, credited with prophecy. Abbotsford, the former home of the poet and novelist Sir Walter Scott, lies just to the west of Melrose. Also in Melrose are Priorwood Garden and Harmony Garden (search for both on www.nts.org.uk). Melrose is also the birthplace of seven-a-side rugby, and hosts the annual Melrose Sevens in April. If you are in Melrose in June, your visit may coincide with the Borders Book Festival (www.bordersbookfestival.org).

The ruins of the 12th-century Melrose Abbey

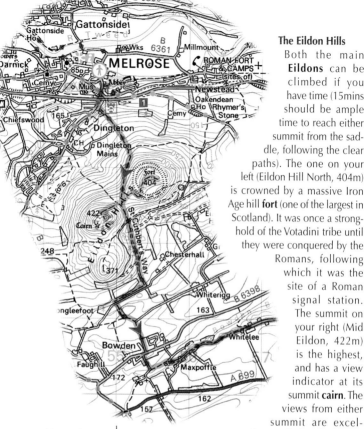

The Eildon Hills

Both the main **Eildons** can be climbed if you have time (15mins should be ample time to reach either summit from the saddle, following the clear paths). The one on your left (Eildon Hill North, 404m) is crowned by a massive Iron Age hill **fort** (one of the largest in Scotland). It was once a stronghold of the Votadini tribe until they were conquered by the Romans, following which it was the site of a Roman signal station. The summit on your right (Mid Eildon, 422m) is the highest, and has a view indicator at its summit **cairn**. The views from either summit are excellent, with the Cheviots to the south and the Lammermuirs to the north. You should also be able to pick out the line of Dere Street, the Roman road followed by SCW in the second half of this stage.

Map continues on page 138

Follow the path down the other side from the saddle, joining a track and bearing L (the path on the R is to the third, lower Eildon). Go L through a gate and into woodland, then veer R. Where the track turns R just before the edge of the wood, keep straight ahead then follow a path

along the edge of the trees. Turn L and descend, cross-ing a farm track, then ascend steps through a plantation to arrive in the village of **Bowden**. There is a prominent octagonal stone well by the road here.

Turn R onto the road, then turn L onto a road sign-posted for SCW and Bowden Kirk. Turn L onto a path where the road veers R. Bowden Kirk can be visited as a short detour, by following the road to the R. ▶ Cross the bridge to the other side of the **Bowden Burn** and turn L, following the true R bank. The path climbs to a track that runs above the valley of the Bowden Burn, and after a short distance you will notice an old stone bridge below you on your L, on what must have been the course of the old road to Bowden.

When the track reaches **Whitelee**, continue straight ahead on the road, passing under a **disused railway line** before arriving at **Newton St Boswells**. Cross the A68 and continue on the road straight ahead, then turn L follow-ing signs for SCW, the Border Abbeys Way and the river. Descend under the bridge carrying the A68 then continue on a path, crossing a bridge over a stream. Bear R (not the path L marked 'To the river') then climb steps to gain a

Crossing the Eildon Hills, near Melrose

There has been a church at this site since the 12th century, although the present building dates mostly from the 17th–18th centuries.

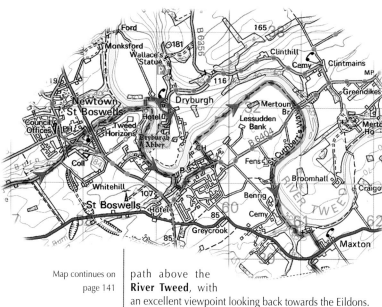

Map continues on page 141

path above the
River Tweed, with
an excellent viewpoint looking back towards the Eildons.
Follow the path down to the Tweed and the Dryburgh
Suspension Bridge, built in 1872.

> The **River Tweed** stretches some 97 miles (156km)
> across southern Scotland and Northumberland, ris-
> ing at Tweed's Well near Foal Burn Head and Bog
> Hill, and emptying into the North Sea at Berwick-
> upon-Tweed. It is internationally known for its fish-
> ing, in particular Atlantic salmon – more of which
> are caught here than on any other river in the EU.
> The Tweed and its catchment rivers have been des-
> ignated a Site of Special Scientific Interest.

> Cross the bridge (note the small classical Temple of
> the Muses on the far side) and turn R, passing a magnifi-
> cent sandstone gateway on your L (built by the 11th Earl
> of Buchan in the early 19th century, as the entrance to
> his orchard), to reach **Dryburgh Abbey** in about 10mins.

> Now a romantic ruin tucked into a bend of the River
> Tweed, **Dryburgh Abbey** was founded in 1150 by

Hugh de Moreville, Constable of Scotland, who invited canons of the Premonstratensian Order from Alnwick in Northumberland. It grew into the main Premonstratensian foundation in Scotland, but was attacked and burnt by English forces several times in the 14th and 16th centuries. The final blow came in 1544 when it was torched, along with much of the rest of Dryburgh, by the Earl of Hertford, and the Reformation finally sealed its fate in 1560. In 1786 it was purchased by David Steuart Erskine, 11th Earl of Buchan, who moved into nearby Dryburgh House. The North Transept Chapel contains the tomb of Sir Walter Scott. For those who wish to stay in Dryburgh, there is the Dryburgh Abbey Hotel (www.dryburgh.co.uk, tel: 01835 822261).

Just north of the village is an enormous sandstone statue of Scottish national hero William Wallace, carved in the early 19th century.

Return to the true R bank of the Tweed and follow the path alongside a bend in the river. After going up and down several sections of wooden steps, turn R and ascend to the village of **St Boswells**. There is a low section of the path here that is prone to flooding after very heavy rainfall. ▶

If there is flooding, follow the road W from the Dryburgh Suspension Bridge and turn L onto the A68, which will take you into St Boswells.

St Boswells was an important centre by the 16th century, although much of it was razed to the ground by the English army in 1544. The surprisingly large village green (known simply as The Green), thought to be the largest in Scotland, is home to an annual livestock fair dating back to the 1600s. This began as a week-long sheep fair, but had become a one-day event (including large numbers of horses and cattle) by the early 19th century. St Boswell's Fair is held on 18 July. The name St Boswells appears to derive from St Boisil, a monk from Melrose Abbey who was an early mentor of St Cuthbert.

The ruins of Dryburgh Abbey

Accommodation is available at the Buccleuch Arms Hotel (www.buccleucharmshotel.co.uk, tel: 01835 822243) and the Old Manse B&B (www.the oldmansemelrose.com, tel: 01835 822047). The 67 bus stops in St Boswells.

Smailholm Tower, a well-preserved 15th-century tower house, is only some 4 miles (6.5km) northeast of St Boswells. From the 17th century, Smailholm Tower, and later the adjacent Sandyknowe, were owned by the Scott family, and it was here that Sir Walter Scott spent part of his childhood recovering from illness.

From the village green in St Boswells, walk E along the main road (B6404) as far as Braeheads Road, opposite a prominent drinking fountain. Turn L onto Braeheads Road, then bear R and follow the edge of the golf course alongside the River Tweed. After passing an area of eroded sandstone on the far bank, cross the road next to the **Mertoun Bridge** (which dates from the 19th century), and continue alongside the river and into woodland. After the cemetery you pass Maxton Church, which is dedicated to St Cuthbert and has a bell dating from the early 1600s. Ascend to the

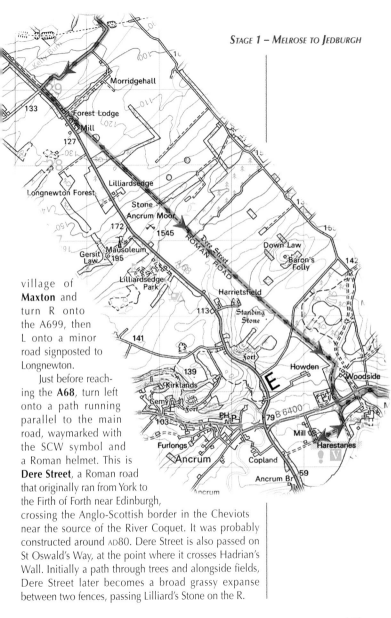

village of **Maxton** and turn R onto the A699, then L onto a minor road signposted to Longnewton.

Just before reaching the **A68**, turn left onto a path running parallel to the main road, waymarked with the SCW symbol and a Roman helmet. This is **Dere Street**, a Roman road that originally ran from York to the Firth of Forth near Edinburgh, crossing the Anglo-Scottish border in the Cheviots near the source of the River Coquet. It was probably constructed around AD80. Dere Street is also passed on St Oswald's Way, at the point where it crosses Hadrian's Wall. Initially a path through trees and alongside fields, Dere Street later becomes a broad grassy expanse between two fences, passing Lilliard's Stone on the R.

Lilliard's Stone is a small monument to a woman who, according to legend, fought bravely in the Battle of Ancrum Moor, which was fought between the Scots and the English near this spot in 1545. There was once a large cross here, erected by the monks of Melrose Abbey, and in the late 14th century representatives of the English and Scottish crowns would come here to attempt to resolve disputes. Beyond Lilliard's Stone and clearly visible on Gersit Law, on the far side of the A68, is the mausoleum of General Sir Thomas Monteath Douglas.

On the horizon ahead of you as you follow Dere Street is the **Waterloo Monument**, a huge 150ft (46m) tower on Peniel Heugh, visible for miles around. It was completed in 1824, after an earlier version of the monument had collapsed. You also pass a lake and wetland area known as Baron's Folly Moss on your left, which has plenty of birdlife. ◀

The lake takes its name from the small building on top of Down Law, Baron's Folly, said to have been built by an unknown baron as a secret meeting place for himself and his lover.

Cross a minor road and enter woodland, passing a trail on the R to Woodside Gardens, a Victorian walled garden that is only a few minutes away (www.woodside garden.co.uk). Cross another road, then follow the path over a wooden bridge and turn R off the main trail towards Harestanes, about 5mins further on.

Harestanes Visitor Centre, a former farm, has exhibitions and events, a gift shop, tea room, nature trail and a large outdoor children's play area (01835 830306, open April–October). The Waterloo Monument can be reached on foot from Harestanes, although the tower itself is not open to the public.

Those staying at Ancrum should follow the drive from Harestanes N to the minor road crossed previously and turn L onto this to the A68. Cross the A68 with care and follow the minor road into Ancrum. In the morning, retrace your steps to Harestanes. Otherwise, those staying at Jedburgh should proceed as follows.

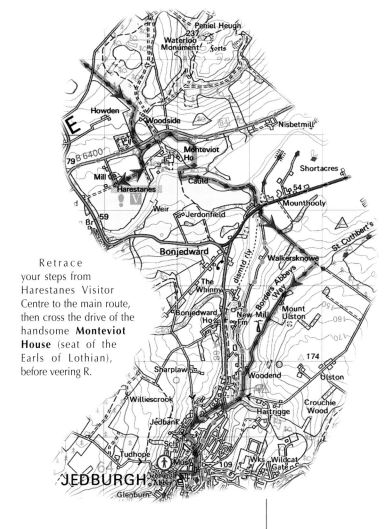

Retrace your steps from Harestanes Visitor Centre to the main route, then cross the drive of the handsome **Monteviot House** (seat of the Earls of Lothian), before veering R.

Monteviot House (www.monteviot.com) was built in 1740, and partially enlarged in the 19th century by the architect Edward Blore (who also worked on Buckingham Palace). The gardens are open to the public during the summer (April–October).

19th-century dovecote in woods near Monteviot House

Turn R again before the **River Teviot**, passing a sign to 'river view' on your L. Look out for the boot scraper next to a tree, and the large 19th-century dovecot, both on your L. The path moves away from the river for a short section, before turning L to reach the suspension bridge, built in 1999 after an earlier bridge was damaged by floods. It is apt to sway a little uncomfortably in the wind. Turn L and follow the river bank, turning R just before reaching the Jed Water, which you follow to the **A698**.

Turn L and follow the main road across the bridge, then take the road on your R. ▸ Bear L and follow the track uphill, with good views back to Peniel Heugh and the Waterloo Monument. Just over ½ mile (1km) after leaving the A698 you reach a junction with the Border Abbeys Way trail on your R. If you have stayed the night in Ancrum and do not intend to visit Jedburgh, keep straight ahead past the Border Abbeys Way trail before turning L as described in Stage 2.

Turn R onto the Border Abbeys Way, and L onto the minor road before reaching the Jed Water and the A68. Cross the main road with care and follow the river path (or simply turn L and follow the main road itself) into the centre of **Jedburgh**.

Continuing along the A698 will bring you to Mounthooly, where you will find the Hoolet's Nest B&B (tel: 01835 850764).

JEDBURGH

Jedburgh first appears in documents in AD864, when a bishop of Lindisfarne established two settlements on the Jed Water, both called Gedwearde. It was sacked or occupied repeatedly over the centuries by English armies as they passed this way – eventually, the Scots destroyed the castle themselves rather than have it keep falling into English hands. Locals often pronounce Jedburgh as 'Jeddart'.

Jedburgh Abbey was founded by David I in 1138, as a priory for canons of the Augustinian order, who had perhaps come from St Quentin Abbey in France. It is exceptionally well preserved (especially when one considers its position so close to the 'troubled' English–Scottish border), with much of the Abbey Church of St Mary the Virgin still standing after almost 900 years. The Abbey Visitor Centre has a good collection of artefacts, including ▸

an ivory comb from around 1100 (search for 'Jedburgh Abbey' on www.historic-scotland.gov.uk).

Other places to visit while in Jedburgh include the fortified house in which Mary Queen of Scots stayed in 1566. She fell seriously ill during her stay, and is said to have commented later when locked in the Tower of London, 'Would that I had died in Jedburgh!'

James Hutton, often considered the father of modern geology, was born in Jedburgh. The distinctive rock formations at nearby Inchbonny – vertical and folded bands of rock surmounted by horizontal bands of sandstone – are among those which led him to challenge conventional notions of geological time in his book *Theory of the Earth* (1788). Inchbonny can be reached by walking south a short distance from the town centre on the A68. Accommodation in Jedburgh includes the Glenbank House Hotel (www.jedburgh-hotel.com, tel: 01835 862258) and Meadhon House B&B (www.meadhon.co.uk, tel: 01835 862504).

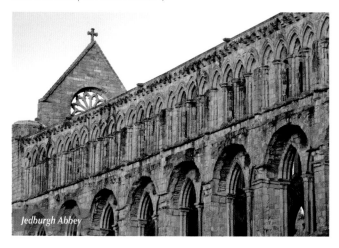

Jedburgh Abbey

STAGE 2

Jedburgh to Kirk Yetholm

Start	Jedburgh Abbey, Jedburgh
Finish	Village green, Kirk Yetholm
Distance	16 miles (26km)
Time	7hrs 45mins
Maps	OS Explorer OL16; OS Landranger 74
Access	The 51 Jedburgh–Edinburgh; 68 Jedburgh–Galashiels; 131 (Mon–Sat) Jedburgh–Newcastle
Accommodation	The Farmhouse at Yetholm Mill; a few alternatives in Kirk Yetholm and Town Yetholm. Accommodation is also available in Morebattle.

This is a moderate day's walking, crossing Wideopen Hill, the highest point on SCW, on the edge of the Cheviots, with good paths and two fairly long stretches of road walking. If preferred, this stage can be broken with a stop at Morebattle.

Retrace your steps from **Jedburgh** along the Border Abbeys Way to the junction with SCW, turn R (SE), then almost immediately take the marked path on the L, leaving Roman Dere Street at this point. The trail passes through attractive woodland, with silver birch and other trees. Turn R at the road, then keep straight ahead on a track where the road veers R. Descend to the bridge over the **Oxnam Water**,

Map continues on page 148

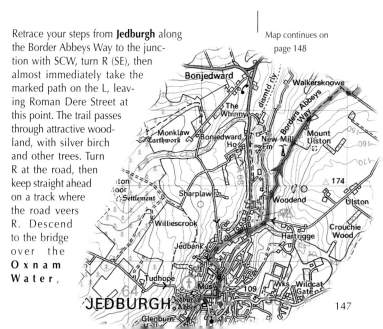

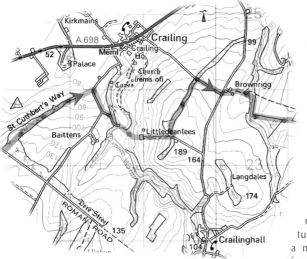

near prominent sandstone cliffs, then continue up the slope beyond. Pass the farmhouses at the top, then keep straight ahead up the road, before turning L into a narrow sliver of woodland just before the top of the hill. Turn R onto a road again, passing **Brownrigg Farm** and continuing alongside fields and through patches of woodland.

The ruins of Cessford Castle, near Morebattle, built in the 15th century

About 4½ miles (7km) after the junction of SCW and the Border Abbeys Way, turn L onto a farm track, soon veering R with excellent views ahead to the ruins

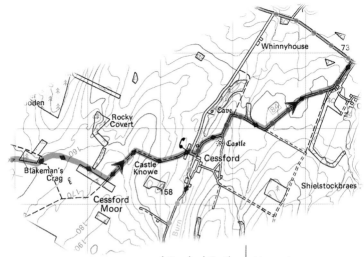

of Cessford Castle, and the Cheviots beyond.

Map continues on page 150

This brings you to **Cessford**, with its pretty row of houses built in 1870. Before this date Cessford was actually a much larger and more important settlement, but following the Enclosure Acts of the late 18th and early 19th centuries, many of the smaller houses were demolished. On reaching the sealed road, head over the bridge, then follow the road around to the L, to reach **Cessford Castle** on your R. Walk up across the field for a better view (but do not enter the building, since the masonry is unstable).

Dating from the mid-15th century (although there was possibly already some form of castle here at least a century earlier), **Cessford Castle** was a stronghold of the Kers, one of the most powerful families in the area. It is a massive and uncompromising structure, clearly built with defence a paramount consideration (the border with England lies only 8 miles (13 km) away) – the walls are over 13ft (around 4m) thick in places. During the 1500s it was besieged several times by the English, and the Kers were also embroiled in an ongoing blood feud with another powerful clan, the Scotts of Buccleuch. The castle was abandoned in 1607.

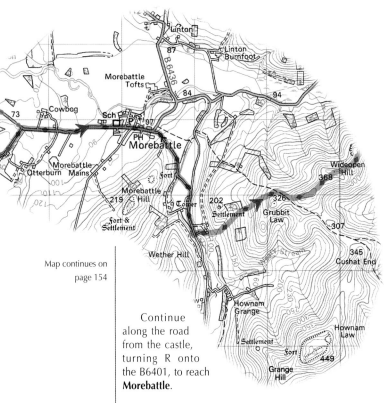

Map continues on
page 154

Continue along the road from the castle, turning R onto the B6401, to reach **Morebattle**.

Morebattle is a small village by the Kale Water, at the foot of the Cheviots. The church dates mostly from the 18th century, with later additions from 1899. An earlier church on this site was destroyed by fire in 1544. The name Morebattle means 'settlement by the lake', referring to Linton Loch, a large area of marshland to the northeast between Morebattle and Linton, which was drained in the 18th century (a small remnant of this still exists below the north flanks of Wideopen Hill, where the B6401 heads over towards Yetholm). Meals and accommodation in Morebattle are available at the Templehall Inn (www.templehallhotel.com, tel: 01573 440249).

According to legend, the nearby village of Linton was the abode of the so-called **Linton Worm**, a medieval dragon (slain by one John de Somerville). The legend bears similarities to that other famous 'worm' of the northeast, the Lambton Worm, upon which Bram Stoker's novel *The Lair of the White Worm* is based.

The route over Grubbit Law and Wideopen Hill between Morebattle and Kirk Yetholm

Head E through the centre of Morebattle, passing the **Templehall Inn** on the R, then taking the smaller road up on your R, with the knobbly hills of the Cheviots ahead. Descend on a road to your L, then turn R onto the road alongside the **Kale Water**. An old tower is just visible hidden in the trees to your R. Pass a ford on your L, then shortly after this turn L and cross the stream on the wooden footbridge.

The Cheviots are the remnants of a massive granite intrusion injected into the earth's crust beneath the volcanoes that stood here some 360 million years ago. Heat generated by the superheated granite of this intrusion hardened the existing lava with which

A view of the Cheviots (with Hownam Law on the right), from the route over Wideopen Hill

it came into contact, and the resulting metamorphosed rock, now eroded, forms a series of rocky tors. Vegetation on the Cheviots is characterised by hardy moor grass, rather than heather. The highest peak, The Cheviot (804m), lies around 5½ miles (9km) south of SCW, just east of the border ridge.

Follow the farm track as it zigzags uphill, then turn R onto a footpath that ascends between two small areas of woodland. The path continues to climb steeply, bringing you just to the L (N) of **Grubbit Law** (326m) and crossing a footpath that heads over Cushat End (345m) to the SE. Head more or less NE over open, blustery tops, with patches of heather moorland bringing splashes of colour to the surrounding hills. The views to the R (SE) are particularly impressive. The striking and very prominent, almost flat-topped hill to the SE is Hownam Law (449m), site of an Iron Age hill fort.

Follow the trail alongside a stone wall, to reach **Wideopen Hill** (368m), which marks both the highest point on St Cuthbert's Way, and the approximate midway point between Melrose and Lindisfarne.

Follow the wall round to the R, then L. Descend steeply (slippery after rain), then ascend slightly, and walk alongside another wall over **Crookedshaws Hill** (306m), before descending steeply again. Turn R then L through fields, to arrive at a track. Turn R onto this and follow it down to the road, which you turn L onto. After ¾ mile (1km) you come to the **B6401**, which you follow for a further ¾ mile (1km) into **Town Yetholm**, passing The Plough Hotel; turn R and cross the bridge to reach **Kirk Yetholm**.

To reach The Farmhouse B&B, keep straight ahead and you will find it on your L; to reach the Border Hotel, either continue up the road beyond The Farmhouse B&B, or take the signed SCW path from just after the bridge, in either case arriving at the village green and the hotel in 5mins.

The history of **Kirk Yetholm** is closely associated with that of the Scottish Gypsies (in particular the Faa family), who had settled here by the end of the 17th century. One theory of their arrival in Yetholm is that they were granted the right to settle here by Sir William Bennet of Marlfield, as a reward for

Monument to the Yetholm Gypsies, next to the village green in Kirk Yetholm

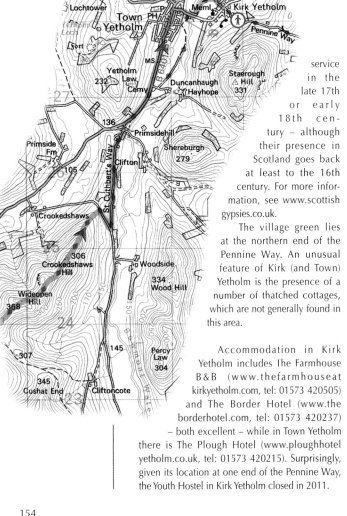

service in the late 17th or early 18th century – although their presence in Scotland goes back at least to the 16th century. For more information, see www.scottish gypsies.co.uk.

The village green lies at the northern end of the Pennine Way. An unusual feature of Kirk (and Town) Yetholm is the presence of a number of thatched cottages, which are not generally found in this area.

Accommodation in Kirk Yetholm includes The Farmhouse B&B (www.thefarmhouseat kirkyetholm.com, tel: 01573 420505) and The Border Hotel (www.the borderhotel.com, tel: 01573 420237) – both excellent – while in Town Yetholm there is The Plough Hotel (www.ploughhotel yetholm.co.uk, tel: 01573 420215). Surprisingly, given its location at one end of the Pennine Way, the Youth Hostel in Kirk Yetholm closed in 2011.

STAGE 3

Kirk Yetholm to Wooler

Start	Village green, Kirk Yetholm
Finish	High Street, Wooler
Distance	13 miles (21km)
Time	6hrs 40mins
Maps	OS Explorer OL16; OS Landranger 74 and 75
Access	The 81, 81A and 81C (Mon–Sat) Kelso–Yetholm
Accommodation	The Tankerville Arms and several alternatives in Wooler; limited accommodation available at Hethpool and (just off-route) Old Yeavering.

This is a reasonably short but fairly strenuous stage spent almost entirely in the Cheviots, crossing the border ridge between Kirk Yetholm and Hethpool, then climbing to more high ground between Yeavering Bell and the Newton Tors. There are good paths, magnificent scenery and around 600m of ascent. It can be broken into two stages by stopping at or just beyond Hethpool.

From the village green in **Kirk Yetholm** take the road uphill signposted to Halterburn, SCW now sharing its route with that of the Pennine Way. Turn L off the road at the

Map continues on page 157

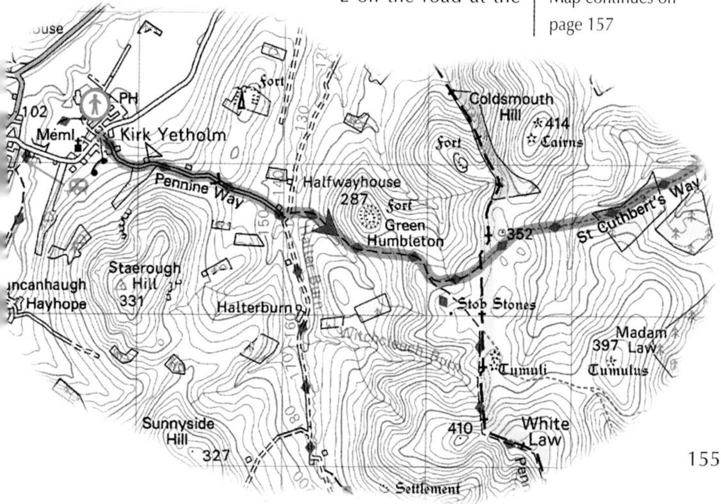

Border fence between England and Scotland

bottom of the hill, crossing the **Halter Burn** and ascending steadily on a clear trail. About ¾ mile (1km) after leaving the road, the trail veers L, leaving the Pennine Way which continues straight ahead. Coninue uphill to the border fence and wall, where twin signs pointing in opposite directions announce 'Welcome to Scotland' and 'Welcome to England'. Cross the stile, casting your eye back for a last look at the way you have come. Then say farewell to Scotland, and step into Northumberland.

Follow the trail straight ahead, ascending slightly – from where a short detour to Eccles Cairn (352m), on your L, gives further enhanced views – then descending, through several boggy patches, to reach a plantation. Walk through and along the edge of the plantation (which is surprisingly dark inside), to arrive at a farm track a short distance after emerging from the trees. Follow the farm track to **Elsdonburn Farm**, turning L between the house and outbuildings and crossing the **Elsdon Burn** by a bridge. Turn R onto a sealed road and follow this down the valley, passing one road on the R. Note the cultivation terraces on the L, on the slopes of White Hill, which may be prehistoric in origin. Turn R onto a pretty tree-lined lane and stroll into the tiny village of **Hethpool**.

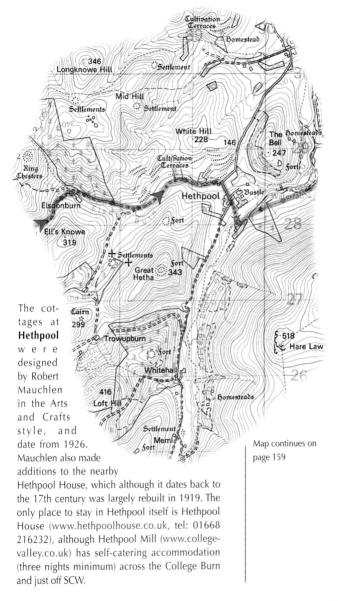

The cottages at **Hethpool** were designed by Robert Mauchlen in the Arts and Crafts style, and date from 1926. Mauchlen also made additions to the nearby Hethpool House, which although it dates back to the 17th century was largely rebuilt in 1919. The only place to stay in Hethpool itself is Hethpool House (www.hethpoolhouse.co.uk, tel: 01668 216232), although Hethpool Mill (www.college-valley.co.uk) has self-catering accommodation (three nights minimum) across the College Burn and just off SCW.

Map continues on page 159

Cottages at Hethpool in the College Valley

Stretching south from Hethpool to The Cheviot is the tranquil **College Valley** (www.college-valley.co.uk), a beautiful and remote area owned and managed by the Sir James Knott Trust. It is an area rich in prehistoric remains, including several hill forts and, just south of Hethpool on the west side of the valley, a Neolithic stone circle. Wildlife in the valley includes feral goats (around 150 of them) and red squirrels. The black grouse was reintroduced successfully a few years back, although recently numbers seem to be in decline. The mountains around the head of the valley still bear the remains of several plane crashes from the Second World War, where aircraft struck the hillsides during bad weather and poor visibility – several of the survivors were rescued by local shepherds. At Mounthooly near the head of the valley (off-route, around 6km south of Hethpool and SCW) there is a YHA bunkhouse (01668 216358).

Follow the marked track through a field in front of the cottages, crossing a bridge over the **College Burn** and

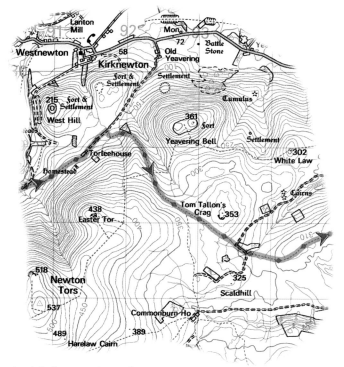

turning L before entering a plantation. As you emerge from the trees, the path crosses a lovely area of moorland with views of Newton Tors on the R and the gorse- and scree-covered The Bell on your L, and Yeavering Bell ahead. ▶ There is a short section of narrow, sometimes slippery path above a stream, which the trail then crosses.

Around this area and on the slopes of the surrounding hills, you may see **feral goats**, which have inhabited this part of the Cheviots for some 150 years. These rather shaggy, long-horned animals were the original domesticated goat in the UK, and would have been kept during the Anglo-Saxon period and earlier, but from the 19th century onwards were gradually replaced by imported breeds, and are now comparatively rare. Herds

Map continues on page 162

A path on the L leads down to Hethpool Linn waterfall, a 5min detour.

The landscape below the Newton Tors, near Hethpool

like this one in the Cheviot Hills almost certainly descend from animals released from captivity in the 19th century.

Pass **Torleehouse Farm** Hethpool, the trail skirting above the farmhouse before joining the gravel farm track just beyond it. Follow this for a short distance then turn R just before a cattle grid, and follow the path uphill and then L. ◄

The trail ascends gradually, crosses a stile and then continues uphill with a wall on the R.

Continuing along the farm track from Torleehouse brings you to Old Yeavering B&B (**www.oldyeavering. co.uk**). Nearby is the site of Ad Gefrin, the seventh-century palace of the Anglo-Saxon kings of Northumbria.

On your L is the bronze-coloured bulk of **Yeavering Bell** (361m), across the twin summits of which lie the remains of the largest and most important hill fort in Northumberland. Dating from the Iron Age, the site consists of the remains of a massive enclosing wall, surrounding an area of some 5.5ha, with numerous circular depressions marking the locations of former buildings.

Pass a trail on the L to Yeavering Bell, then veer L, passing the prominent rocks of **Tom Tallon's Crag** (353m) on your L. The wall that you reach soon after this is said to have been built from the stones of a Bronze Age cairn in the 19th century. Pass a small plantation on your L, joining a track briefly before crossing a small stream and continuing on a path across open moorland. On meeting another wall, turn L and continue alongside it roughly ENE. Veer L and then R, passing **Gains Law** (319m) and **Humbleton Hill** (298m) on your L, and a series of sheepfolds.

Yeavering Bell in the Cheviot Hills, site of the largest Iron Age hill fort in Northumberland

Humbleton Hill and the area just south of Gains Law, known as the Trows, provide some of the best examples of sub-glacial meltwater channels in northern England, for which reason they have been listed as a SSSI. Humbleton Hill was itself the site of an Iron Age hill fort. The Battle of Humbleton Hill – mentioned in the opening scene of Shakespeare's *Henry IV Part I* – was fought between the English

161

(under Henry Percy, also known as 'Harry Hotspur') and the Scots in 1402 just north of here.

Descend further, with the town of Wooler spread out below you, then enter an area of woodland. Head down through the trees to emerge onto one of the educational trails of **Wooler Common**. Turn R to the car park and information boards (the road on the L, Common Road, would also lead you down into Wooler), then veer R alongside a small stream with a plantation on your L. At the corner of the plantation, go through a gate (no waymarkings) onto open moorland, then bear L to reach the far corner of the plantation. Follow the path through the trees, then descend over more open heath, bearing R and passing through a boggy area before reaching the unsealed road by **Waud House**. Follow this down to the houses on the western edge of town, descending Common Road then Ramsey Lane to reach the High Street in **Wooler**.

WOOLER

Often described as the gateway to the Cheviots, Wooler is a traditional old market town with 18th- and 19th-century housing clustered in the valley below Humbleton Hill. The remains of the castle lie off Church Street, near a war memorial. The Youth Hostel, just south of the High Street, was purpose built in 1943 to house the local WLA (Women's' Land Army), formed to provide agricultural labour following conscription of male farmworkers into the armed forces in the Second World War.

The author Virginia Woolf and her husband, Leonard, stayed here for a month in 1914 (lodging at the Tankerville Arms). Leonard commented, 'I am inclined to think that the Cheviots are the loveliest country in England… There is an extraordinary stillness and peace in their forms; and nowhere in the world is the light and colour of sky and earth more lovely than in this bit of England.' Fair praise.

There are shops and pubs in the High Street; the Tankerville Arms (www. tankervillehotel.co.uk, tel: 01668 281581), a landmark old coaching inn, is diagonally across the A697 at the bottom of Ryecroft Way (which leads off the northern end of the High Street). The 267 and 464 buses to Berwick-upon-Tweed depart from Wooler.

The Cheviots near Tom Tallon's Crag, looking down towards the area known as the Trows

STAGE 4

Wooler to West Mains/Fenwick

Start	High Street, Wooler
Finish	Lindesfarne Inn, West Mains or Manor House B&B, Fenwick
Distance	13 miles (21.5km) to West Mains; 11½ miles (19km) to Fenwick
Time	5hrs 25mins (West Mains); 5hrs (Fenwick)
Maps	OS Explorer 340; OS Landranger 75
Access	The 267 and 464 Berwick-upon-Tweed–Wooler buses
Accommodation	The Lindisfarne Inn at West Mains; Manor House B&B at Fenwick; limited options at Beal and, less conveniently, in West Kyloe.

With paths, tracks and some road walking this is an easy stage, which crosses Weetwood Moor and visits St Cuthbert's Cave, before descending towards the coast through Shiellow Wood.

From **Wooler** High Street, descend Church Street, passing St Mary's Church (18th century) and the war memorial, and cross the A697. Cross the bridge over Wooler Water and turn R along a street that follows the course of the dismantled Alnwick–Cornhill Railway.

The **Alnwick–Cornhill Railway** was a 36-mile (58km), single-track line, opened in 1887. Unable to compete with increasing local bus services, it closed to passengers in the 1930s, although it remained in operation for freight until 1965. The station at Wooler has been converted into two private houses, the trackbed between the platforms having been filled up to platform level. The goods shed is on the A697, just north of the junction with Church Street, and is now an antiques market.

If the lions on the gateposts look rather Venetian, that is because they were made by Italian POWs, when this was a World War II prison camp.

Turn L onto Brewery Road, passing a school on your L. ◄ Follow the road uphill then take the marked

footpath on your L, with good views
back over Wooler, nestled
below the Cheviots.
The trail now crosses
the attractive
open moorland
of **Weetwood
Moor**.

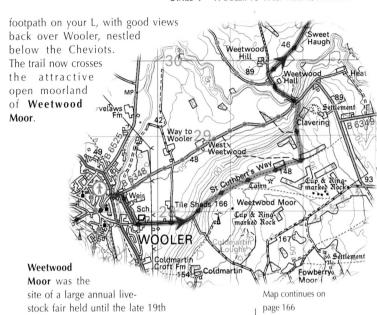

**Weetwood
Moor** was the
site of a large annual livestock fair held until the late 19th

Map continues on
page 166

*Wooler on the edge of the Cheviot Hills,
viewed from the trail to Weetwood Moor*

165

Weetwood bridge, dating from the 16th century

century, called the Whitsun Tryst (from which the area is gets its local name of Whitsun Bank). There are also several prehistoric sites on Weetwood Moor, including stones with cup-and-ring marks. Some of the cup-and-ring-marked stones can be visited by veering right where the path forks.

Veer L where the path splits into two, passing a small plantation on your L. Turn L through a gate just before

Map continues on page 168

reaching a second plantation,

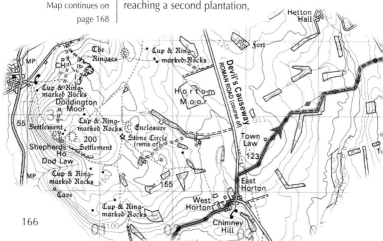

166

then pass another plantation on your L, with excellent views of the Till Valley and the attractive Weetwood Bridge. Descend towards the bridge, taking the R of two paths, and cross the road carefully. The bridge dates from the 16th century and was restored in the 18th century, then again in 2005.

Cross the bridge and follow the road uphill, passing **Weetwood Hall**, then following the road as it bends around to the R. N of here is Doddington Moor, an area rich in prehistoric remains, including numerous cup-and-ring-marked rocks, the remains of a stone circle and of several settlements. According to local legend, St Cuthbert tended sheep in this area during his childhood. As you follow the road NE you will pass two poles that mark the course of a natural gas pipeline from the North Sea.

Walk past the houses of **West Horton** and **East Horton**, turning L onto a road sometimes known as the Devil's Causeway, which follows the course of an old Roman road. Turn R onto an unsealed road, with views of Greensheen Hill to the NE, and passing an old World War II pillbox on your R before descending to cross the

Fields beside the Devil's Causeway, a Roman road near East Horton

167

Hetton Burn. Pillboxes are a familiar sight along the Northumberland coast (there is another on the edge of the small wood on the rise ahead of you), this having been the expected site of a possible land invasion of Britain by Hitler's Germany. Bear L then R, ascending then crossing a sealed road, and passing Hazelrigg B&B (www.hazelriggbandb.com) on your R.

Continue uphill, then turn L onto a footpath just after a plantation, where the road veers R. Walk alongside the plantation before turning R through a stile, then L above gorse and alongside the edge of the field. Pass the corner of the large wood, keeping along the edge of the field, then turn R onto a track that ascends towards the woods ahead, with the sandstone crags of Cockenheugh visible through a gap in the trees. On meeting the wood turn L, until you

reach the clear path on your R leading up to **St Cuthbert's Cave**.

St Cuthbert's Cave is a beautiful sandstone overhang, forming a natural shelter. According to popular belief, monks from

Lindisfarne, forced to leave the island in the face of repeated Viking raids, rested here with the body of St Cuthbert and other precious relics in AD875.

Return to the main track and continue to the edge of the woods, then turn R and ascend to the top of the rise, on the shoulder of **Greensheen Hill**. Ahead across the fields is the course of St Oswald's Way, passing just below Fawcett Hill, with Virgin Hill Woods to the R of this.

On my most recent visit to this area (November 2011) there was a proposal to build 16 **wind turbines** in the area below you, including between the edge of St Cuthbert's Wood and the course of St Oswald's Way. As well as sitting on the course of three long-distance footpaths, SCW, SOW and the NCP, and obstructing the hitherto unspoilt view of the coast, these would be clearly visible from Northumberland Coast AONB (including Holy Island) and would almost certainly have a negative impact on birdlife, including important migrant species such as greylag and pink-footed geese (Holburn Lake and Moss, just

St Cuthbert's Cave, where monks fleeing from Lindisfarne Priory are said to have sheltered with the remains of St Cuthbert

On the trail to St Cuthbert's Cave

on the other side of Greensheen Hill, is a SPA and a RAMSAR site). You can find more details at www. middletonburnactiongroup.co.uk.

Descend across the fields (one of the two gates at the bottom was jammed on my last visit) then ascend again, to meet SOW and the NCP coming in from the R. Here you get your first, breathtaking view of the coast around Holy Island – one which can be enhanced by hiking up to the high ground just off the route on your R.

To continue

For the remainder of the stage to **West Mains** or **Fenwick**, and the final sections of SCW to Holy Island and up the coast to Berwick-upon-Tweed (Stages 5 and 6), see St Oswald's Way Stages 6–8. Fenwick is reached 3 miles (5km) from the junction with SOW; West Mains is a further 1½ miles (2.5km).

APPENDIX A

Route summary table

St Oswald's Way

Stage	Start	Finish	Distance	Time	Maps
1	Heavenfield or Wall	Kirkwhelpington	17½ miles (28.5km); 19 miles (31km) from Wall	8hrs 15mins; 8hrs 45mins from Wall	OS Explorer OL42, OL43 and 316; OS Landranger 87 and 81
2	Kirkwhelpington	Rothbury	15 miles (24km)	6hrs	OS Explorer OL42; OS Landranger 81
3	Rothbury	Warkworth	18 miles (29km)	8hrs	OS Explorer 325 and 332; OS Landranger 81
4	Warkworth	Craster	13½ miles (21.5km)	5hrs 20mins	OS Explorer 332 and 340; OS Landranger 75 and 81
5	Craster	Bamburgh	14 miles (22km)	5hrs	OS Explorer 332; OS Landranger 81
6	Bamburgh	West Mains or Fenwick	14½ miles (23.5km) to West Mains; 13 miles (21km) to Fenwick	7hrs (West Mains); 6hrs 35mins (Fenwick)	OS Explorer 340; OS Landranger 75
7	West Mains or Fenwick	Holy Island	7½ miles (12km) from West Mains; 6 miles (9.5km) from Fenwick	2hrs 45mins from West Mains; 2hrs 20mins from Fenwick	OS Explorer 340; OS Landranger 75
8	Holy Island	Berwick-upon-Tweed	13 miles (20.5km)	5hrs 30mins	OS Explorer 340 and 341; OS Landranger 75

St Cuthbert's Way

Stage	Start	Finish	Distance	Time	Maps
1	Melrose	Jedburgh	19½ miles (32km)	8hrs 15mins	OS Explorer 338 and OL16; OS Landranger 73
2	Jedburgh	Kirk Yetholm	16 miles (26km)	7hrs 45mins	OS Explorer OL16; OS Landranger 74
3	Kirk Yetholm	Wooler	13 miles (21km)	6hrs 40mins	OS Explorer OL16; OS Landranger 74 and 75
4	Wooler	West Mains or Fenwick	13 miles (21.5km) to West Mains; 11½ miles (19km) to Fenwick	5hrs 25mins (West Mains); 5hrs (Fenwick)	OS Explorer 340; OS Landranger 75

For the rest of the SCW see SOW Stages 7–8.

Northumberland Coast Path

Stage	Start	Finish	Distance	Time	Maps
1	Cresswell	Warkworth	10½ miles (16.5km)	3hrs 30mins	OS Explorer 335 and 332; OS Landranger 81

For the rest of the NCP see SOW Stages 4–8.

APPENDIX B

Glossary and pronunciation

bell	hill
brig	bridge
burn	stream
cleugh	ravine
coble	traditional open-top Northumberland fishing boat
flother	area of marsh or bog
harr	mist in coastal areas
haugh	low, level pasture or marshy area
heugh	crag, cliff or steep-sided hill
kirk	church
knowe	(pronounced 'now') low hill
law	hill
linn	waterfall
lonnen	lane
lough	(pronounced 'luff') shallow freshwater lake
moss	marshy or boggy area

pele	fortified tower
rigg	ridge
sike	stream
skerr (plural *skerries*)	rock outcropping into the sea, small rocky reef
snook	headland or point
stane	stone
steading	small farm settlement

The pronunciation of the following place names is also worth noting:

Alnmouth	'Allenmouth'
Alnwick	'Annick'
Boulmer	'Boomer'
Fenwick	'Fennick'
Jedburgh	sometimes pronounced 'Jeddart'
Yetholm	'Yettom'

At 368m, Wideopen Hill (between Morebattle and Kirk Yetholm) is the highest point on St Cuthbert's Way

APPENDIX C
Accommodation

St Oswald's Way

Hexham
The Station Inn
Station Road, Hexham NE46 1EZ
Tel: 01434 603155
www.stationinnhexham.co.uk

The Beeches B&B
40 Leazes Park, Hexham NE46 3AY
Tel: 01434 605900
www.bandbhexham.com

Wall
The Hadrian Hotel
Front Street, Wall NE46 4EE
Tel: 01434 681232
www.hotel-hadrians-wall.com

Kirkwhelpington
Cornhills Farmhouse B&B (1½ miles (2.5km) off-route)
Cornhills, Kirkwhelpington NE19 2RE
Tel: 01830 540232
www.northumberlandfarmhouse.co.uk

Great Tosson (1½ miles (2.5km) off-route if climbing Simonside)
Tosson Tower Farm
Great Tosson, Rothbury NE65 7NW
Tel: 01669 620228
www.tossontowerfarm.com

Rothbury
The Queen's Head
Townfoot, Rothbury NE65 7SR
Tel: 01669 620470
www.queensheadrothbury.com

Linhope House B&B
Walby Hill, Rothbury NE65 7NT
Tel: 01669 622843
www.linhopehouse.co.uk

Springfield Guest House
Townfoot, Rothbury NE65 7BA
Tel: 01669 621277
www.springfieldguesthouse.co.uk

Weldon Bridge

The Angler's Arms
Weldon Bridge NE65 8AX
Tel: 01665 570271
www.anglersarms.com

Felton

River Cottage B&B
Mouldshaugh Farm, Felton NE65 9NP
Tel: 01670 787081
www.river-cottage-bandb.co.uk

Warkworth

Warkworth House Hotel
16 Bridge Street, Warkworth NE65 0XB
Tel: 01665 711276
www.warkworthhousehotel.co.uk

Tower House B&B
47 Castle St, Warkworth NE65 0UN
Tel: 01665 714375
www.towerhousebandb.co.uk

Alnmouth

The Red Lion
22 Northumberland St, Alnmouth NE66 2RJ
Tel: 01665 830584
www.redlionalnmouth.com

Beaches B&B
56 Northumberland St, Alnmouth NE66 2RJ
Tel: 01665 830006
www.beachesbyo.co.uk

Boulmer

The Fishing Boat Inn
14–15 Beach View, Boulmer NE66 3BP
Tel: 01665 577750
www.thefishingboatinn.co.uk

Craster

Harbour Lights B&B
Whin Hill, Craster NE66 3TP
Tel: 01665 576062
www.harbourlights-craster.co.uk

The Cottage Inn (½ mile (800m) off-route)
Dunstan Village, Craster NE66 3SZ
Tel: 01665 576658
www.cottageinnhotel.co.uk

Stonecroft B&B (½ mile (800m) off-route)
Dunstan Village, Craster NE66 3SZ
Tel: 01665 576433
www.stonecroft-craster.co.uk

Low Newton-by-the-Sea

The Ship Inn
Low Newton-by-the-Sea NE66 3EL
Tel: 01665 576262
www.shipinnnewton.co.uk

Beadnell

The Craster Arms
The Wynding, Beadnell NE67 5AX
Tel: 01665 720272
www.crasterarms.co.uk

Seahouses

Bamburgh Castle Inn
Seahouses NE68 7SQ
Tel: 01665 720283
www.bamburghcastleinn.co.uk

The Olde Ship Inn
Seahouses NE68 7RD
Tel: 01665 720200
www.seahouses.co.uk

Springhill (½ mile (800m) off-route)
Springhill Farm
Seahouses NE68 7UR
Tel: 01665 721820
www.springhill-farm.co.uk

Bamburgh

The Victoria Hotel
Front Street, Bamburgh NE69 7BP
Tel: 01668 214431
www.victoriahotel.net

The Sunningdale Hotel
21–23 Lucker Road, Bamburgh NE69 7BS
Tel: 01668 214334
www.sunningdale-hotel.com

Glenander B&B
27 Lucker Road, Bamburgh NE69 7BS
Tel: 01668 214336
www.glenander.com

Belford

Blue Bell Hotel
Market Place, Belford NE70 7NE
Tel: 01668 213543
www.bluebellhotel.com

The Old Vicarage B&B
1 North Bank, Belford NE70 7LY
Tel: 01668 213025
www.belfordoldvicarage.co.uk

Fenwick

The Manor House B&B
Fenwick TD15 2PQ
Tel: 01289 381016
www.manorhousefenwick.co.uk

West Mains/Beal

Lindisfarne Inn
West Mains, Beal TD15 2PD
Tel: 01289 381223
www.lindisfarneinn.co.uk

Brock Mill Farmhouse B&B
Beal TD15 2PB
Tel: 01289 381283
www.holyislandaccommodation.com

Holy Island

The Crown & Anchor
The Market Place, Holy Island TD15 2RX
Tel: 01289 389215
www.holyislandcrown.co.uk

The Lindisfarne Hotel
Holy Island TD15 2SQ
Tel: 01289 389273
www.thelindisfarnehotel.co.uk

Manor House Hotel
Holy Island TD15 2RX
Tel: 01289 389207
www.manorhouselindisfarne.com

Bamburgh View B&B
Fenkle Street, Holy Island TD15 2SR
Tel: 01289 389212
www.lindisfarne.org.uk/bamburghview

The Bungalow B&B
Holy Island TD15 2SE
Tel: 01289 389308
www.thebungalowholyisland.co.uk

For more accommodation on Holy Island see
www.lindisfarne.org.uk/accommodation.htm

Cheswick/Goswick

East House B&B (½ mile (800m) off-route)
Cheswick TD15 2RW
Tel: 07799 775795
www.easthousebedandbreakfast.co.uk

Berwick-upon-Tweed

1 Sallyport Hotel
1 Sallyport (off Bridge Street), Berwick-upon-Tweed TD15 1EZ
Tel: 01289 308827
www.sallyport.co.uk

The Cobbled Yard Hotel
40 Walkergate, Berwick-upon-Tweed TD15 1DJ
Tel: 01289 308407
www.cobbledyardhotel.com

The Walls B&B
8 Quay Walls, Berwick-upon-Tweed TD15 1HB
Tel: 01289 330233
www.thewallsberwick.com

Berwick-upon-Tweed YHA
Dewars Lane Granary, Dewars Lane, Berwick-upon-Tweed TD15 1HJ
Tel: 0845 371 9676
www.yha.org.uk/hostel/berwick

Northumberland Coast Path

Amble
Harbour Guesthouse B&B
24–26 Leazes Street, Amble NE65 0AA
Tel: 01665 710381
www.harbourguesthouseamble.co.uk

St Cuthbert's Way

Melrose
The George & Abbotsford Hotel
High Street, Melrose TD6 9PD
Tel: 01896 822308
www.georgeandabbotsford.co.uk

The Old Bank House B&B
27 Buccleuch Street, Melrose TD6 9LB
Tel: 01896 823712
www.oldbankhousemelrose.co.uk

Dryburgh
Dryburgh Abbey Hotel
Dryburgh, St Boswells TD6 0RQ
Tel: 01835 822261
www.dryburgh.co.uk

St Boswells
Buccleuch Arms Hotel
The Green, St Boswells TD6 OEW
Tel: 01835 822243
www.buccleucharmshotel.co.uk

The Old Manse B&B
Main Street, St Boswells TD6 0BB
Tel: 01835 822047
www.theoldmansemelrose.com

Ancrum (1 mile (1.5km) off-route)
Cheviot View B&B
The Green, Ancrum, Jedburgh TD8 6XA
Tel: 01835 830563
www.cheviotview.btinternet.co.uk

Mounthooly (¼ mile (300m) off-route)
The Hoolet's Nest
Mounthooly, Jedburgh TD8 6TJ
Tel: 01835 850764

Jedburgh
Glenbank House Hotel
Castlegate, Jedburgh TD8 6BD
Tel: 01835 862258
www.jedburgh-hotel.com

Meadhon House B&B
48 Castlegate, Jedburgh TD8 6BB
Tel: 01835 862504
www.meadhon.co.uk

Morebattle
Templehall Hotel
Main Street, Morebattle TD5 8QQ
Tel: 01573 440249
www.templehallhotel.com

Kirk Yetholm
The Farmhouse at Yetholm Mill
Kirk Yetholm
Tel: 01573 420505
www.thefarmhouseatkirkyetholm.com

The Border Hotel
The Green, Kirk Yetholm TD5 8PQ
Tel: 01573 420237
www.theborderhotel.com

The Plough Hotel
Main Street, Town Yetholm TD5 8RS
Tel: 01573 420215
www.ploughhotelyetholm.co.uk

Hethpool
Hethpool House B&B
Hethpool NE71 6TW
Tel: 01668 216232
www.hethpoolhouse.co.uk

Kirknewton (½ mile (800m) off-route)
Old Yeavering B&B
Old Yeavering, Kirknewton, Wooler NE71 6HF
Tel: 07771 911 259
www.oldyeavering.co.uk

Wooler
The Tankerville Arms Hotel
Wooler NE71 6AD
Tel: 01668 281581
www.tankervillehotel.co.uk

Tilldale House B&B
34/40 High Street, Wooler NE71 6BG
Tel: 01668 281450
www.tilldalehouse.co.uk

Wooler YHA
30 Cheviot St, Wooler NE71 6LW
Tel: 0845 371 9668
www.yha.org.uk/hostel/wooler

Hazelrigg (near **East Horton**)
Hazelrigg B&B
The Old School, Hazelrigg, Chatton NE66 5SA
Tel: 01668 215246
www.hazelriggbandb.com

For accommodation for West Mains/Fenwick and from Holy Island to Berwick-upon-Tweed, see St Oswald's Way.

APPENDIX D
Useful contacts

Tourist information

Visit Northumberland
www.visitnorthumberland.com

Visit Northeast England
www.visitnortheastengland.com

Northumberland Coast
www.northumberlandcoastaonb.org
www.northumberland-coast.co.uk

Northumberland National Park
www.northumberlandnationalpark.org.uk

Northumberland Wildlife Trust
www.nwt.org.uk

Hadrian's Wall Country
www.hadrians-wall.org

Lindisfarne
www.lindisfarne.org.uk

Visit Scotland
www.visitscotland.com

Borders Tourist Board
www.borderstouristboard.com

Undiscovered Scotland
www.undiscoveredscotland.co.uk

Local tourist information offices
Northumberland

Alnwick tel: 01665 511333
Berwick-upon-Tweed tel: 01289 301780
Craster tel: 01665 576007
Hexham tel: 01434 652220
Morpeth tel: 01670 535200
Rothbury tel: 01669 620887
Seahouses tel: 01289 301777
Wooler tel: 01668 282123

Borders

Jedburgh tel: 01835 863170
Melrose tel: 01896 822283

Walks – online resources

St Oswald's Way
www.stoswaldsway.com

St Cuthbert's Way
www.stcuthbertsway.fsnet.co.uk

Northumberland National Park
www.northumberlandnationalpark.org.uk

Northumberland Coast
www.northumberland-coast.co.uk

North Sea Trail
www.northseatrail.org

Cheviot Walks
www.cheviotwalks.co.uk

Safe crossing times for Holy Island

Northumberland County Council
www.northumberland.gov.uk; click on
Leisure, Tourism & Culture followed by
Holy Island Tide Times.

Wildlife and heritage tours

Northern Experience Wildlife Tours
Tel: 01670 827465
www.northernexperiencewildlifetours.co.uk

Farne Islands boat trips
Tel: 01665 720308
www.farne-islands.com

Guided/self-guided walking holidays and luggage services

Shepherd Walks
Tel: 01830 540453
www.shepherdswalks.co.uk

Sherpa Van
Tel: 0871 5200124
www.sherpavan.com

Transport operators

East Coast Trains
www.eastcoast.co.uk

National Rail Enquiries
www.nationalrail.co.uk

Arriva
www.arrivabus.co.uk

Traveline
www.traveline.info

Glen Valley Tours
Tel: 01668 281578
www.glenvalley.co.uk

Perryman's Buses
Tel: 01289 308719
www.perrymansbuses.co.uk

Munros of Jedburgh
Tel: 01835 862253
www.munrosofjedburgh.co.uk

Advanced Taxis (covers the Northumberland and Tynedale areas, including Hexham and Hadrian's Wall)
Tel: 01434 606565
www.advancedtaxis.com

Maps and guidebooks

The Map Shop
www.themapshop.co.uk

Ordnance Survey
www.ordnancesurvey.co.uk

Natural History Bookshop
www.nhbs.com

Stanfords
www.stanfords.co.uk

Shepherd Walks
www.shepherdswalks.co.uk

Northumberland County Council
www.northumberland.gov.uk

Sustrans
www.sustransshop.co.uk

Other

Ad Gefrin (archaeology of the Cheviot Hills)
www.gefrin.com

Bridges on the Tyne
www.bridgesonthetyne.co.uk

Disused Stations (disused railway lines and stations)
www.disused-stations.org.uk

England's North East
www.englandsnortheast.co.uk

National Trails
www.nationaltrail.co.uk

Northern Cross (Easter pilgrimage walks)
www.northerncross.co.uk

Northumberland Rock Art
rockart.ncl.ac.uk

Roman Britain
www.roman-britain.org

St Oswald's Hospice
www.stoswaldsuk.org

Scottish Gypsies
www.scottishgypsies.co.uk

Sites of Special Scientific Interest (England)
www.sssi.naturalengland.org.uk

Sites of Special Scientific Interest (Scotland)
www.snh.gov.uk/protecting-scotlands-nature/protected-areas/national-designations/sssis

Trinity House (lighthouses)
www.trinityhouse.co.uk

Walter Scott Digital Archive
www.walterscott.lib.ed.ac.uk

APPENDIX E
Further reading

St Oswald's Way, St Cuthbert's Way and the Northumberland Coast Path

There are very few guides covering St Oswald's Way and St Cuthbert's Way in any detail, and these are listed below. Neither of the 'official' guides for these routes includes information on accommodation, unfortunately. Note that the (non-OS) maps in the St Oswald's Way official guidebook (and those in the Short Walks guide) are not always clear enough to use without carrying the relevant OS sheets.

Martin Paminter, *St Oswald's Way: The Official Guidebook* (Alnwick County Council, 2011)

Martin Paminter, *Short Walks Around St Oswald's Way* (Alnwick County Council, 2009)

Ron Shaw, *St Cuthbert's Way: The Official Guide* (2nd edition; Birlinn, 2011)

Ronald Turnbull, *St Cuthbert's Way* (Rucksack Readers, 2010)

Iain Robson, *Northumberland Coast Path* (Northumberland County Council, 2007)

Other guidebooks

Paddy Dillon, *The Pennine Way* (3rd edition; Cicerone, 2010)

Alan Hall, *Walking in Northumberland* (2nd edition; Cicerone, 2004)

Gemma Hall, *Slow Northumberland and Durham* (Bradt, 2012)

Tony Hopkins, *Northumberland: The Official National Park Guide* (David & Charles, 2002)

Mary Low, *St Cuthbert's Way: A Pilgrim's Companion* (Wild Goose Publications, 2000)

Mark Richards, *Hadrian's Wall Path* (2nd edition; Cicerone, 2010)

History, art and architecture

Bede, *The Age of Bede* (Penguin, 2004)

Bede, *The Ecclesiastical History of the English Church and People* (Penguin, 1991)

Stan Beckensall, *Northumberland's Hidden History* (Amberley, 2009)

Stan Beckensall, *Prehistoric Rock Art of Northumberland* (The History Press, 2001)

Stan Beckensall, *Northumberland: Shadows of the Past* (NPI Media, 2005)

PH Blair, *Northumbria in the Days of Bede* (Victor Gollancz, 1976)

William Brockie, *The Gypsies of Yetholm* (Rutherford, 1884)

Michelle P Brown, *The Lindisfarne Gospels and the Early Medieval Period* (British Library, 2010)

Michelle P Brown, *The Lindisfarne Gospels: Society, Spirituality and the Scribe* (British Library, 2003)

Michelle P Brown, *Painted Labyrinth: The World of the Lindisfarne Gospels* (British Library, 2003)

Tom Cadwallender (ed.), *Exploring the Historic Buildings of the Northumberland Coast Area of Outstanding Natural Beauty* (Northumberland County Council, 2006)

J Campbell, *The Anglo-Saxons* (Penguin, 1991)

D Dixon, *Upper Coquetdale* (R Redpath, 1904)

Keith Durham, *Strongholds of the Border: Fortifications of the Anglo-Scottish Border 1296–1603* (Osprey, 2008)

DH Farmer, *The Oxford Dictionary of Saints* (Oxford, 2003)

Richard Fawcett, *Scottish Abbeys and Priories* (Historic Scotland, 1993)

Paul Frodsham, *Archaeology in Northumberland National Park* (Council for British Archaeology, 2004)

PA Graham, *Highways and Byeways in Northumbria* (Macmillan, 1920)

Kitty Kruft, John Dunbar and Richard Fawcett, *The Buildings of Scotland: The Borders* (Yale, 2006)

Nikolaus Pevsner and Ian Richmond, *The Buildings of England: Northumberland* (Yale, 2002)

Eric Robson, *The Border Line: The Story of the England–Scotland Border* (Frances Lincoln, 2007)

David Rollason, *Northumbria, 500–1100: Creation and Destruction of a Kingdom* (Cambridge, 2007)

FM Stenton, *Anglo-Saxon England* (Oxford, 1946)

AV Tokely, *The Kirk Yetholm Gypsies* (Hawick Archaeological Society, 2004)

Margaret Tynedale, *Legends and Folklore of Northumbria* (Collins, 1930)

Wildlife and plants

Marjorie Blamey and Richard Fitter, *Wild Flowers of Britain and Ireland* (A & C Black, 2003)

Tom Cadwallender (ed.), *Bird Watching on the Northumberland Coast Area of Outstanding Natural Beauty and Heritage Coast* (Northumberland County Council, 2007)

Tom Cadwallender (ed.), *Exploring the Plantlife of the Northumberland Coast Area of Outstanding Natural Beauty* (Northumberland County Council, 2006)

Wendy Dickson, *The Wildflowers of Coastal Northumberland: A Photographic Guide* (Keepdate, 2000)

Simon Harrap and David Nurney, *RSPB Pocket Guide to British Birds* (A & C Black, 2007)

Ian Kerr, *The Birds of Holy Island* (2nd edition; Ian Kerr, 2007)

Jane Lancaster, *Exploring the Shore in Northumberland and Berwickshire* (Northumberland County Council, 2004)

Jane Lancaster, *The Underwater World of Northumberland and Berwickshire* (Northumberland County Council, 2006)

Paul Sterry, *Collins Complete Guide to British Birds* (Collins, 2008)

GA Swan, *Flora of Northumberland* (Natural History Society of Northumbria, 1993)

Geology

Clive Crossley and Tom Cadwallender, *Explore the Geology and Landscape of the Northumberland Coast AONB* (Northumberland County Council, 2007)

Elizabeth Pickett, Gill Thompson et al., *Ancient Frontiers: Exploring the Geology and Landscapes of the Hadrian's Wall Area* (British Geological Survey & Northumberland National Park Authority, 2006)

P Stone, D Millward and B Young, *Northern England* (Regional Geology Guides) (British Geological Survey, 2010)

Photographs

Derry Brabbs, *Hadrian's Wall* (Francis Lincoln, 2008)

Roger Clegg and Mark Richards, *The Spirit of Hadrian's Wall* (Cicerone Press, 2008)

Joe Cornish, *The Northumberland Coast* (Francis Lincoln, 2008). There really is no more beautiful photographic portrait of the Northumberland coast than this.

Lee Frost, *Northumbria* (Constable, 1998)

David Taylor, *St Cuthbert's Way: A Photographic Journey* (Blurb, 2011)

Literature

AJ Cronin, *The Stars Look Down* (Victor Gollancz, 1935)

Kevin Crossley-Holland (ed.), *The Anglo-Saxon World: An Anthology* (Oxford, 2009)

Rowena Farre, *A Time from the World* (Hutchinson, 1962)

Richard Hamer (ed.), *A Choice of Anglo-Saxon Verse* (Faber, 2006)

Kathleen Raine, *Farewell Happy Fields* (Hamish Hamilton, 1973)

Robert Westall, *The Machine Gunners* (Penguin, 1975)

NOTES

LISTING OF CICERONE GUIDES

BRITISH ISLES CHALLENGES, COLLECTIONS AND ACTIVITIES

The End to End Trail
The Mountains of England and Wales
  1 Wales & 2 England
The National Trails
The Relative Hills of Britain
The Ridges of England, Wales and Ireland
The UK Trailwalker's Handbook
The UK's County Tops
Three Peaks, Ten Tors

MOUNTAIN LITERATURE

Unjustifiable Risk?

UK CYCLING

Border Country Cycle Routes
Cycling in the Hebrides
Cycling in the Peak District
Cycling the Pennine Bridleway
Mountain Biking in the Lake District
Mountain Biking in the Yorkshire Dales
Mountain Biking on the South Downs
The C2C Cycle Route
The End to End Cycle Route
The Lancashire Cycleway

SCOTLAND

Backpacker's Britain
  Central and Southern Scottish Highlands
  Northern Scotland
Ben Nevis and Glen Coe
Great Mountain Days in Scotland
North to the Cape
Not the West Highland Way
Scotland's Best Small Mountains
Scotland's Far West
Scotland's Mountain Ridges
Scrambles in Lochaber
The Ayrshire and Arran Coastal Paths
The Border Country
The Cape Wrath Trail

The Great Glen Way
The Isle of Mull
The Isle of Skye
The Pentland Hills
The Southern Upland Way
The Speyside Way
The West Highland Way
Scotland's Far North
Walking in the Cairngorms
Walking in the Ochils, Campsie Fells and Lomond Hills
Walking in Torridon
Walking Loch Lomond and the Trossachs
Walking on Harris and Lewis
Walking on Jura, Islay and Colonsay
Walking on Rum and the Small Isles
Walking on the Isle of Arran
Walking on the Orkney and Shetland Isles
Walking on Uist and Barra
Walking the Corbetts
  1 South of the Great Glen
Walking the Galloway Hills
Walking the Lowther Hills
Walking the Munros
  1 Southern, Central and Western Highlands
  2 Northern Highlands and the Cairngorms
Winter Climbs Ben Nevis and Glen Coe
Winter Climbs in the Cairngorms
World Mountain Ranges: Scotland

NORTHERN ENGLAND TRAILS

A Northern Coast to Coast Walk
Backpacker's Britain
  Northern England
Hadrian's Wall Path
The Dales Way
The Pennine Way
The Spirit of Hadrian's Wall

NORTH EAST ENGLAND, YORKSHIRE DALES AND PENNINES

Great Mountain Days in the Pennines

Historic Walks in North Yorkshire
South Pennine Walks
St Oswald's Way and St Cuthbert's Way
The Cleveland Way and the Yorkshire Wolds Way
The North York Moors
The Reivers Way
The Teesdale Way
The Yorkshire Dales
  North and East
  South and West
Walking in County Durham
Walking in Northumberland
Walking in the North Pennines
Walks in Dales Country
Walks in the Yorkshire Dales
Walks on the North York Moors – Books 1 & 2

NORTH WEST ENGLAND AND THE ISLE OF MAN

Historic Walks in Cheshire
Isle of Man Coastal Path
The Isle of Man
The Lune Valley and Howgills
The Ribble Way
Walking in Cumbria's Eden Valley
Walking in Lancashire
Walking in the Forest of Bowland and Pendle
Walking on the West Pennine Moors
Walks in Lancashire Witch Country
Walks in Ribble Country
Walks in Silverdale and Arnside
Walks in the Forest of Bowland

LAKE DISTRICT

Coniston Copper Mines
Great Mountain Days in the Lake District
Lake District Winter Climbs
Lakeland Fellranger
  The Central Fells
  The Mid-Western Fells
  The Near Eastern Fells
  The Northern Fells

The Cathar Way
The GR5 Trail
The Robert Louis Stevenson
   Trail
Tour of the Oisans: The GR54
Tour of the Queyras
Tour of the Vanoise
Trekking in the Vosges and Jura
Vanoise Ski Touring
Walking in Provence
Walking in the Cathar Region
Walking in the Cevennes
Walking in the Dordogne
Walking in the Haute Savoie
   North & South
Walking in the Languedoc
Walking in the Tarentaise and
   Beaufortain Alps
Walking on Corsica

GERMANY
Germany's Romantic Road
Walking in the Bavarian Alps
Walking in the Harz Mountains
Walking the River Rhine Trail

HIMALAYA
Annapurna
Bhutan
Everest: A Trekker's Guide
Garhwal and Kumaon: A
   Trekker's and Visitor's Guide
Kangchenjunga: A Trekker's
   Guide
Langtang with Gosainkund and
   Helambu: A Trekker's Guide
Manaslu: A Trekker's Guide
The Mount Kailash Trek
Trekking in Ladakh

ICELAND AND GREENLAND
Walking and Trekking in
   Iceland
Trekking in Greenland

IRELAND
Irish Coastal Walks
The Irish Coast to Coast Walk
The Mountains of Ireland

ITALY
Gran Paradiso
Italy's Sibillini National Park
Shorter Walks in the Dolomites
Through the Italian Alps
Trekking in the Apennines

Trekking in the Dolomites
Via Ferratas of the Italian
   Dolomites: Vols 1 & 2
Walking in Abruzzo
Walking in Sardinia
Walking in Sicily
Walking in the Central Italian
   Alps
Walking in the Dolomites
Walking in Tuscany
Walking on the Amalfi Coast
Walking the Italian Lakes

MEDITERRANEAN
Jordan – Walks, Treks, Caves,
   Climbs and Canyons
The Ala Dag
The High Mountains of Crete
The Mountains of Greece
Treks and Climbs in Wadi
   Rum, Jordan
Walking in Malta
Western Crete

NORTH AMERICA
British Columbia
The Grand Canyon
The John Muir Trail
The Pacific Crest Trail

SOUTH AMERICA
Aconcagua and the Southern
   Andes
Hiking and Biking Peru's Inca
   Trails
Torres del Paine

SCANDINAVIA
Walking in Norway

SLOVENIA, CROATIA AND
MONTENEGRO
The Julian Alps of Slovenia
The Mountains of Montenegro
Trekking in Slovenia
Walking in Croatia

SPAIN AND PORTUGAL
Costa Blanca: West
Mountain Walking in Southern
   Catalunya
The Mountains of Central
   Spain
The Northern Caminos
Trekking through Mallorca
Walking in Madeira
Walking in Mallorca

Walking in the Algarve
Walking in the Canary Islands:
   East
Walking in the Cordillera
   Cantabrica
Walking in the Sierra Nevada
Walking on La Gomera and
   El Hierro
Walking on La Palma
Walking on Tenerife
Walks and Climbs in the Picos
   de Europa

SWITZERLAND
Alpine Pass Route
Canyoning in the Alps
Central Switzerland
The Bernese Alps
The Swiss Alps
Tour of the Jungfrau Region
Walking in the Valais
Walking in Ticino
Walks in the Engadine

TECHNIQUES
Geocaching in the UK
Indoor Climbing
Lightweight Camping
Map and Compass
Mountain Weather
Moveable Feasts
Outdoor Photography
Polar Exploration
Rock Climbing
Sport Climbing
The Book of the Bivvy
The Hillwalker's Guide to
   Mountaineering
The Hillwalker's Manual

MINI GUIDES
Avalanche!
Navigating with a GPS
Navigation
Pocket First Aid and Wilderness
   Medicine
Snow

For full information on all
our guides, and to order
books and eBooks, visit our
website:
www.cicerone.co.uk.

Walking – Trekking – Mountaineering – Climbing – Cycling

Over 40 years, Cicerone have built up an outstanding collection of 300 guides, inspiring all sorts of amazing adventures.

 Every guide comes from extensive exploration and research by our expert authors, all with a passion for their subjects. They are frequently praised, endorsed and used by clubs, instructors and outdoor organisations.

All our titles can now be bought as **e-books** and many as iPad and Kindle files and we will continue to make all our guides available for these and many other devices.

Our website shows any **new information** we've received since a book was published. Please do let us know if you find anything has changed, so that we can pass on the latest details. On our **website** you'll also find some great ideas and lots of information, including sample chapters, contents lists, reviews, articles and a photo gallery.

It's easy to keep in touch with what's going on at Cicerone, by getting our monthly **free e-newsletter**, which is full of offers, competitions, up-to-date information and topical articles. You can subscribe on our home page and also follow us on **Facebook** and **Twitter**, as well as our **blog**.

Cicerone – the very best guides for exploring the world.

CICERONE

2 Police Square Milnthorpe Cumbria LA7 7PY
Tel: 015395 62069 info@cicerone.co.uk
www.cicerone.co.uk